D0795785

Algrove Publishing Limited
1090 Morrison Drive
Ottawa, Ontario
Canada K2H 1C2

National Library of Canada Cataloguing in Publication Data

Worst, Edward F. (Edward Francis), 1866-1949.
Coping saw work

(Classic reprint series)
Reprint of Coping saw work for elementary manual training
published: Milwaukee, Wis. : Bruce Pub., c1927.
ISBN 1-894572-45-9

1. Woodwork (Manual training). 2. Wooden toy making—Amateurs' manuals. 3. Woodwork—Patterns—Amateurs' manuals. I. Title. II. Title: Coping saw work for elementary manual training. III. Series: Classic reprint series (Ottawa, Ont.)

TT185.W677 2001 684'.082 C2001-904297-3

Printed in Canada
#11201

Publisher's Note

Edward Worst was one of the most prolific writers of woodworking texts in the first half of the 20th century. Although in a senior administrative position in the education system for much of his career, his love of woodworking and of the methods of teaching it generated a number of textbooks for school woodworking courses. The genesis of some of today's most collectible folk art items can be found in *Coping Saw Work*. Similarly, the roots of many of the projects in modern books on scroll saw work will be found in this volume.

Leonard G. Lee
Ottawa
November, 2001

COPING SAW WORK

for Elementary Manual Training

EDWARD F. WORST

Director of

Elementary and Junior-High-School Manual Training and Elementary Construction Work

CHICAGO, ILLINOIS

THE BRUCE PUBLISHING COMPANY

MILWAUKEE, WISCONSIN

INTRODUCTION

The purpose of this manual is to suggest to teachers of the elementary and middle grades, problems in coping saw work and toymaking that are attractive and educative.

The work is so planned that it may be carried on in the regular classroom without an elaborate equipment, thus bringing it within reach of all who desire to pursue an industrial course.

The work is of such a variety and adaptable to both girls and boys that it may very profitably be carried on in the sixth, seventh, and eighth grades of schools not having a regular shop course in manual training.

The work, if carried on in a regular way, will lay a foundation for the more advanced shopwork and also aid in constructing many practical problems to be used in the school and home.

EDWARD F. WORST

Chicago, January 4, 1927

TABLE OF CONTENTS

COPING SAW WORK FOR ELEMENTARY MANUAL TRAINING

Introductory

It is universally agreed that it becomes more difficult every year for a boy upon leaving school to be well equipped to face the battles of life.

It is very essential that teachers and parents should offer every opportunity to help the boy to make his education as complete as possible. To attain this object it is necessary to select such lines of work as will be attractive to the boy and at the same time train his faculties of accuracy, steadiness, and industry. With this end in view, light woodwork presents itself as one of the finest lines of work for training the hand and eye.

The great possibilities of light woodwork are so apparent that it will at once appeal to every class of amateur workers. It lends itself to toy-furniture making, the construction of toy barns, houses, sheds, etc., the making of jointed and movable toys, and small articles useful about the home.

The working equipment required involves but little expense, thus bringing it within reach of all who desire it. The purpose of this chapter is to suggest such exercises as may be constructed in the regular classrooms.

The work, when properly followed, leads to originality on the part of the boy. He learns to make his own drawings and to do his own coloring. In this way he is led into the more advanced work of the upper grades.

Light Woodwork

In the following suggestions for coping saw work, no attempt has been made to furnish a limited series of exercises to be mechanically followed by teacher and pupils. The chief purpose is to give teachers an idea of what fourth and fifth grade pupils are capable of doing, with the hope they will become interested in this intensely attractive line of work for boys.

In the beginning there can be no serious objection to the use of suggestive problems as given in this manual.

Each exercise in light wood should be preceded by a lesson in drawing, whether free hand or mechanical.

The pupils have had considerable experience in the drawing of squares and rectangles as well as circles, in their lower grade work. The time has come when the experience there gained may be applied to the light wood.

Great care should be exercised in not allowing pupils to undertake exercises so difficult in their construction that the work cannot be well done. The work of fourth grade pupils should be confined to problems in two dimensions, in other words, "flat work." This may mean exercises in one piece, or it may mean exercises involving several pieces to be assembled, as in jointed animals.

If the work of the fourth grade is well done, fifth grade pupils have little or no difficulty in undertaking problems based on the box form. Such a series of problems embraces the construction of chairs, tables, wagons, sleds, cradles, etc.

Equipment

The equipment needed for light woodwork is very simple, and includes only a small number of tools, and these, being of the most elementary kind, may be handled very easily by small children.

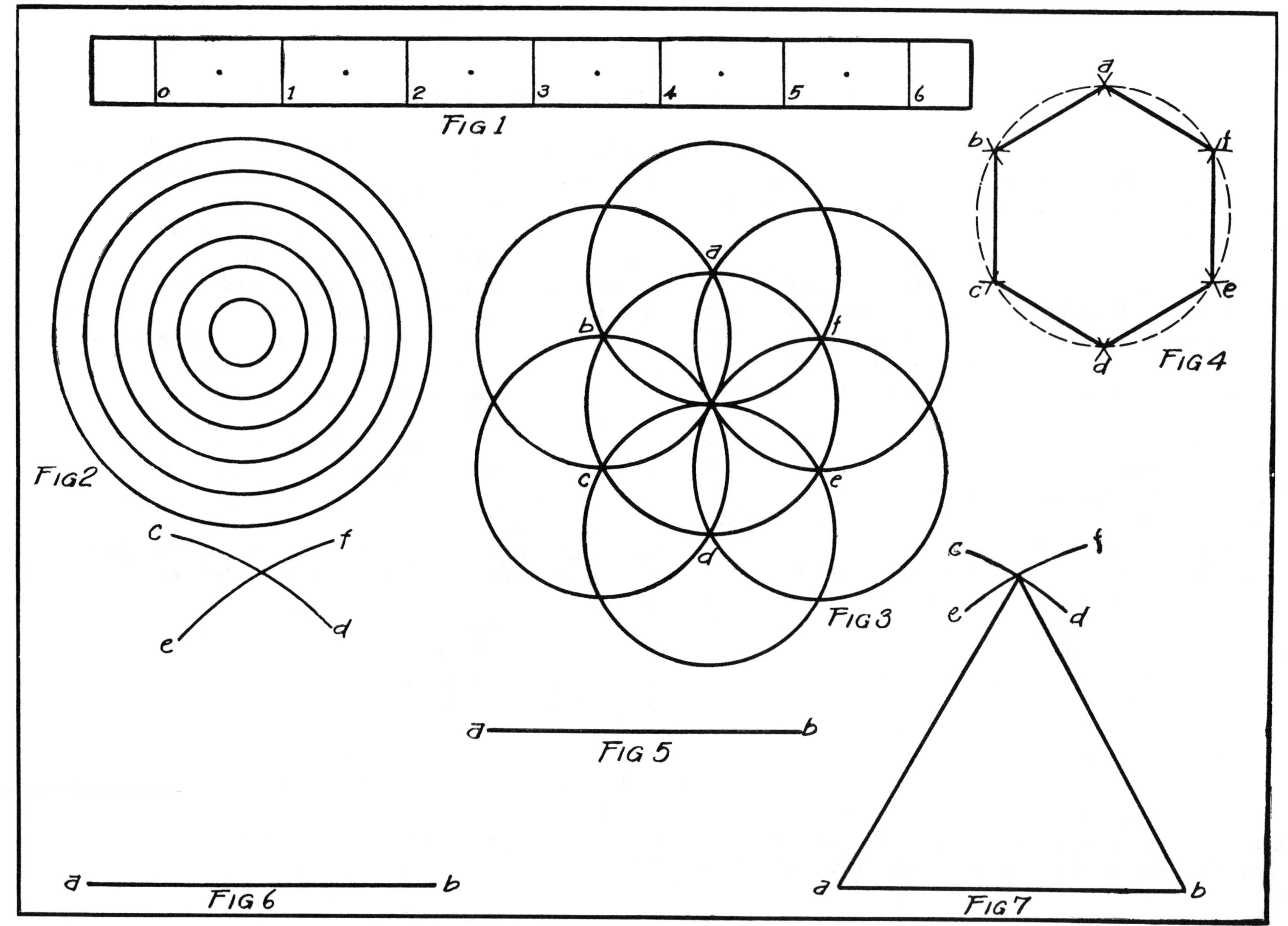

Plate 1—Geometric Forms Made With Compasses and Straight Edge.

Each child should be provided with the following individual set of tools:

1 coping or scroll saw complete.
1 bench pin or sawing board.
1 brad awl.
1 small claw hammer—5 oz.
1 half round file, 6 inch.
1 small iron clamp, 4 inch.
1 cloth board to protect desk top.

If each child is provided with the above set, it will not be necessary for him to disturb his classmates by borrowing tools from them. He will stay at his own bench and take more pains in keeping his set of tools in good condition. Each child is then responsible for the tools in his set.

The following suggests an equipment of general tools:

3 pairs of side cutting pliers—5 inch.
6 rat tail files—8 inch.
3 nail sets.
6 try squares.
1 cross cut saw.
1 rip saw.
1 brace.
1 small iron vise, movable.
6 pair small compasses.
6 dowel bits—one 3/16 inch; three ¼ inch; one ⅜ inch; one ½ inch.

Supplies such as the following should be kept on hand:

Sandpaper, fine and coarse.
Oil paints or dry colors—all colors.
Shellac.
Rivet burrs.
Cotter pins—1 inch by 3/32 inch.
Dowel rods—1 inch and ¼ inch.
3/16 inch or ¼ inch basswood, 3/16 inch or ¼ inch three-ply stock.
Iron brads—all sizes to 1 inch in length.
Tracing paper and carbon paper.
Liquid glue.

Circle Maker

If the school is supplied with compasses, use them. If not, construct the circle maker shown in Fig. 1.

With the paper cutter, cut strips of strawboard ½ inch wide, and any length more than 7 inches. Mark and cut away surplus material as in Fig. 1, leaving the circle maker 7 inches long and ½ inch wide. The dots mark the half inches while the continuous vertical lines mark the whole inches. The half inch at each end is simply a surplus, which makes it possible to use full 6 inches of the maker, if desired. With a pin, puncture each dot and the center of each vertical line. With a small punch, a hole is placed at one end, as in Fig. 1. The hole is for the lead pencil point.

Before beginning a definite drawing, allow the pupils to experiment in the drawing of circles. Develop diameter, radius, circumference. Lead them to see that when a 6 inch circle is asked for, only 3 inches on the circle maker are needed, this being the radius. When doing light woodwork always keep the desk covered with heavy clothboard to protect the top from scratches and other injury.

From the center of a 9 inch by 12 inch piece of drawing paper, draw a 6 inch circle. Do this by forcing a pin through the vertical line 3 inches from the hole at the end. The pin is now forced through the drawing paper and into the clothboard on the top of the desk. Place the pencil point in the hole and swing the circle maker by pulling on the pencil. Using the same center, inscribe a 5 inch circle within the one just drawn.

Using the same center, draw a 4 inch, a 3 inch, a 2 inch and a 1 inch circle within the 6 inch circle. Fig. 2.

The boys will thoroughly enjoy this work. It furnishes most excellent mathematical ideas. It is good elementary mechanical drawing and leads to the drawings necessary for the light woodwork.

Pass to each pupil a 9 inch by 12 inch sheet of manila drawing paper and from the center draw a 4 inch circle. On the upper edge of the circle at a point "a" as a center and with the same radius as the one with which the first circle was drawn, draw another 4 inch circle. The second circle intersects the first circle at the points "b" and "f." Draw another 4 inch circle with its center at "b." This gives another point "c." Draw another 4 inch circle with "c" as its center. Continue these operations until seven complete circles have been drawn. This will give the geometric form shown in Fig. 3. If the teacher so desires, the pupils may color the above exercises with any medium at hand, holding to tints of the same color.

Pass to each pupil a 9 inch by 12 inch piece of drawing paper. With the necessary equipment allow them to make and color an original drawing in circles.

The drawing of Fig. 3 immediately suggests a method for drawing a hexagon. Draw a circle with a 2 inch radius. Choose a point on the circumference of this circle, as "a" in Fig. 4. With the point "a" as a center and with the same 2 inch radius mark the points "b" and "f." With this same radius and "b" as a center locate the point "c." In this same manner locate the points "d" and "e." Connect these points as shown in Fig. 4, and a true hexagon is the result.

The drawing of circles leads the pupil to the drawing of equilateral triangles. Draw a horizontal line 6 inches long (Fig. 5), and letter one end "a" and the other "b." With "a" as a center and with 6 inches on the circle maker, or compass, begin to draw as though an entire circle were wanted. However, only draw the arc "cd" shown in Fig. 6. Stop at this point and develop the arc. If the pupils understand that any part of the circumference of a circle is called an arc, that will be sufficient for the grade.

With "b" as a center, and 6 inches on the circle maker, or compass, draw a second arc, "ef," passing through or intersecting "cd," as shown in Fig. 6. Connect the point "a" and the point where the two arcs intersect, and we have Fig. 7, an equilateral triangle.

With a 4 inch line as a base, construct an equilateral triangle (Fig. 8). Bisect each edge of the triangle. With 2 inches on the circle maker and points "a," "b" and "c" as centers, draw arcs as in Fig. 9.

Pass a 9 inch by 12 inch piece of drawing paper to each pupil and allow him to make an original drawing, combining the circle and equilateral triangle.

STRING WINDER

Draw a rectangle 3½ inches by 2 inches as shown by the dotted lines in Fig. 10. Letter the lines as indicated. With "ab" as a base, draw the intersecting arcs as shown at "e." This is done just as though an equilateral triangle were to be constructed. With the point of intersection "e" as a center, draw the arc "ab." With "cd" as a base, draw the arcs intersecting at "f." With this point of intersection as a center, draw the arc "cd."

With "ac" as a base, draw the arcs intersecting at "h." With this point of intersection as a center, draw the arc "ac." With "bd" as a base, draw the arcs intersecting at "g." With the point of intersection "g" as a center, draw the arc "bd." Cut along the continuous lines, and a pattern for a string winder is the result. This pattern may now be transferred to the wood.

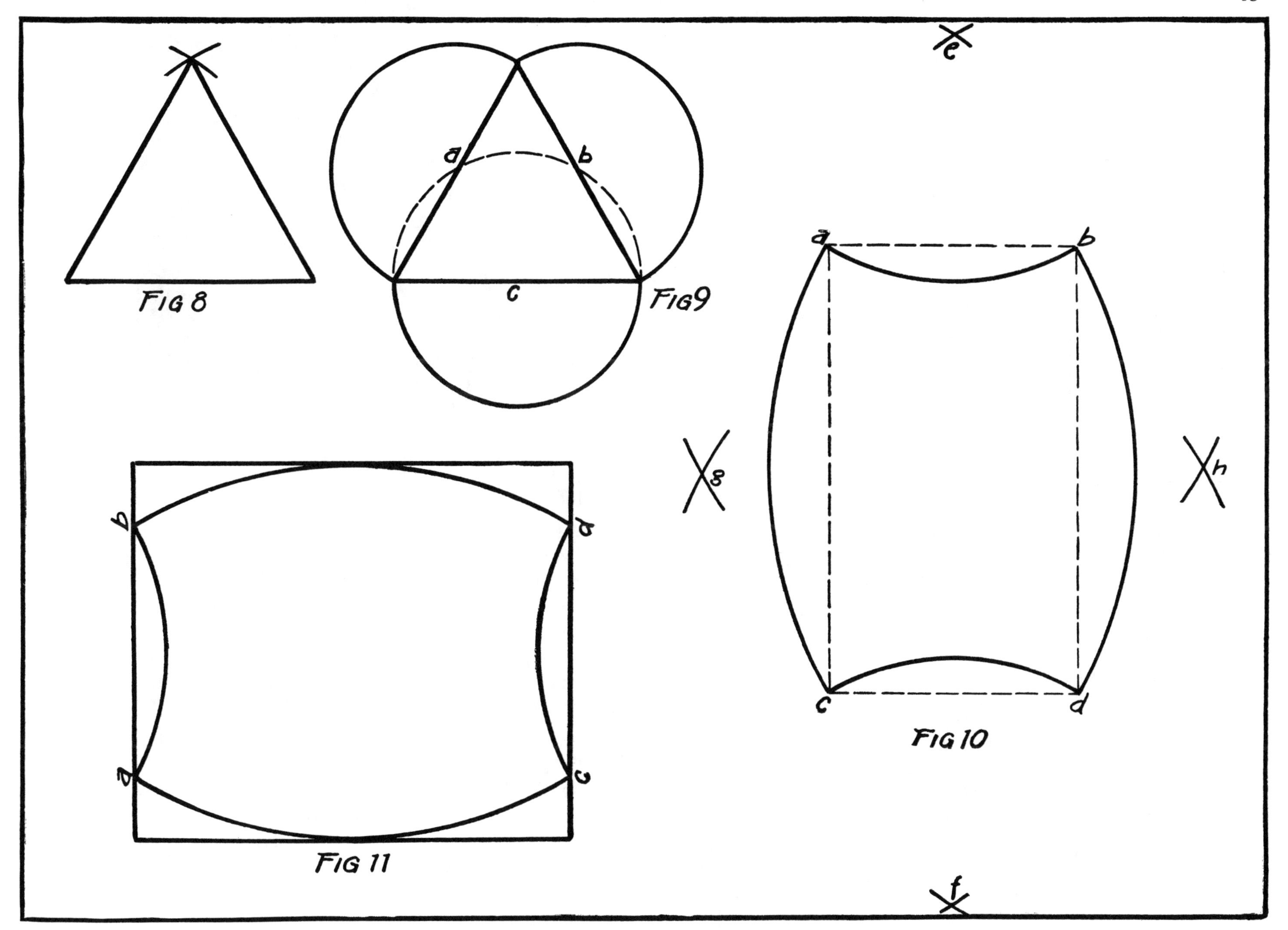

Plate 2—Elementary Mechanical Drawing Done With Compasses and Straight Edge.

The Wood

The lumber, or wood, to be used for this lesson is a piece of basswood, 3/16 inches by 3 inches by 3½ inches.

In naming the dimensions of a piece of lumber, thickness is given first, width second, and length third. The symbol ″ means inches and ′ means feet. The sign "x" means "by"; and the expression 3/16″x3″x3½″, is read, three-sixteenths of an inch thick by three inches wide, by three and one-half inches long. It might be well for the pupils to know what the expression S 2S means. It is a short way of saying surfaced or planed on two

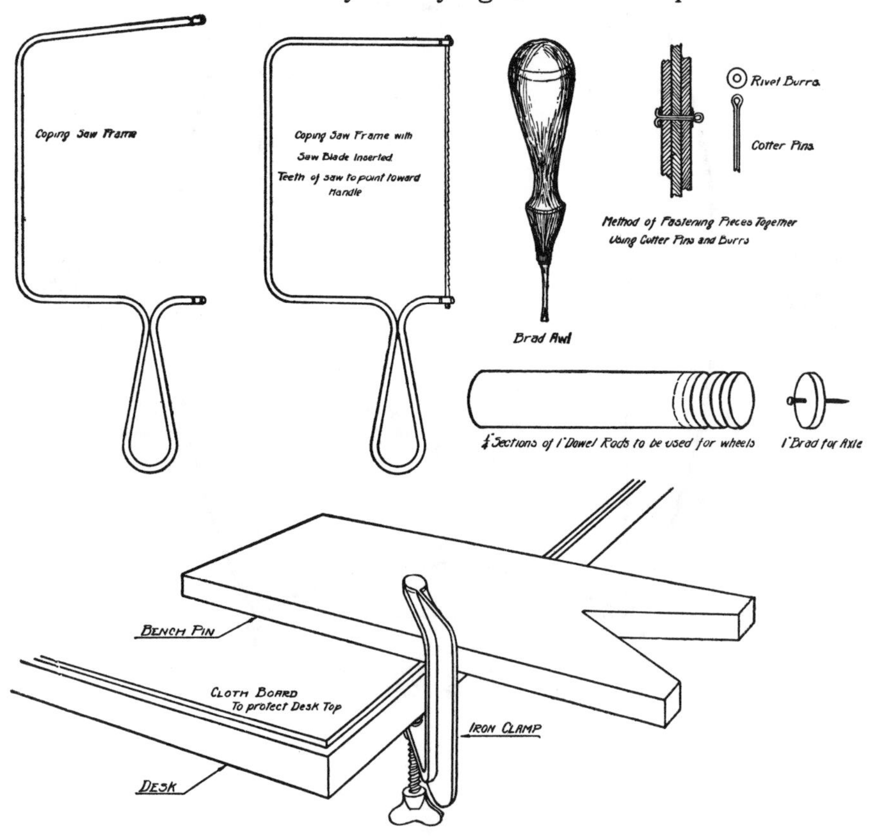

Plate 3—Necessary Equipment for Coping Saw Work.

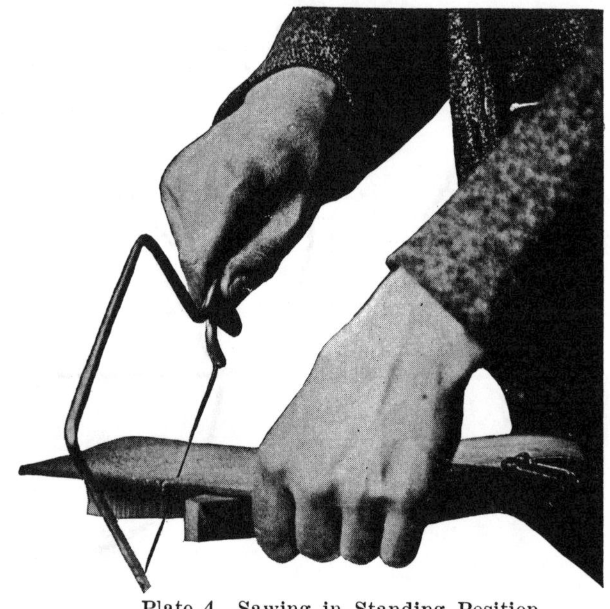

Plate 4—Sawing in Standing Position.

sides,—that is, the piece of lumber is already smooth on the two flat sides.

First: The paper pattern may be cut and placed on the wood and traced around.

Second: A piece of carbon paper, black side down, may be fastened upon the 3/16″x3″x3½″ board with two thumb tacks or dabs of paste at the corners. Place the drawing upon the carbon paper and parallel with the grain of the wood. With the pencil, sketch carefully over the lines of the drawing, thus transferring it to the board.

Be sure that every part of the design is transferred before removing the carbon paper.

Fig. 2, Plate 2, shows the drawing of the string winder as it appears on the light wood. Before beginning the work of sawing, it might be well to make a few statements in regard to the scroll, or coping saw and the way it is used.

Plate 5—Child Sawing When Seated.

The Coping Saw

The coping saw, sometimes called a scroll saw, shown in Plate 3, is used for cutting curves. As the blades of the coping saw are very delicate, it will be necessary to handle them carefully. Before having the pupils use the saw, examine it closely. If the pupil is to stand while doing his sawing, the saw teeth must point away from the handle. This position causes the saw to cut on the downward movement, the child pushing the saw. Plate 4.

If the pupil is to sit and must hold his work on the sawing board, as is the case when the work is carried on in the regular classroom, the teeth of the saw must point toward the handle. The saw in this position does the sawing on the downward movement. The child pulls the saw downward thus making it easy to hold the work. (Plate 5.)

Changing Position of Saw Blade

The position of the saw blade is easily changed by holding the handle of the saw frame against the body and pulling the farther side of the frame toward the handle. (Plate 6.) This will loosen the blade, which may be removed. It will be observed that there are slots in the side, as well as in the ends of the saw frame. The blade is placed in these side slots when long lines are to be sawed.

While the sawing is in operation, the work should be held on the sawing board, which is clamped to the right side of the desk top so that it extends into the aisle. (Plate 5.) The board in this position makes it possible for pupils to hold work with the left hand and to do the sawing with the right hand.

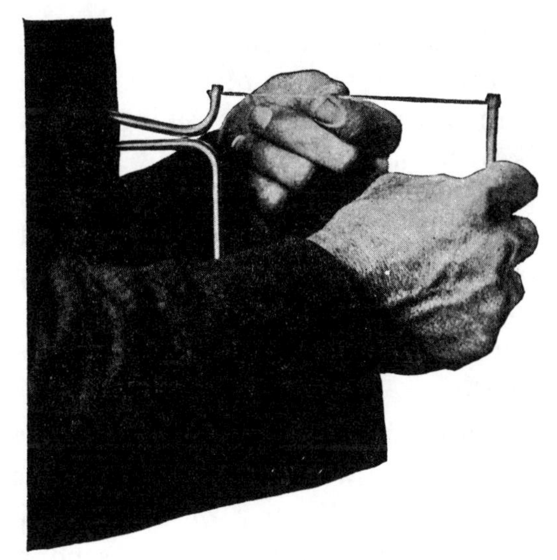

Plate 6.

To Saw String Winder

Place the board upon the sawing board, shown in Plate 3, and begin to work by sawing off the part outside of the curved lines.

In sawing, use short easy strokes, without pressing on the saw. Saw slowly, and be careful to saw just outside of the lines and at exactly right angles to the board—that is, endeavor to keep each end of the saw blade square with the work. (Fig 5.) It will be necessary to shift the position of the board a number of times before the sawing of the outline is completed. Be careful to have that part of the board to be sawed, on, or as near as possible to the small circle in the sawing board. This will prevent the board from being broken. Do not try to hurry.

Files

If the school is not equipped with files, have the pupils make substitutes in the following way:

Flat File: From 3/16″ basswood, saw two ¾″x7″ pieces, To do this it will be necessary to place the saw blade in the side slots so that there may be continuous sawing. If this is not done, the wood strikes the saw frame, making it impossible to continue the sawing. Around one of the pieces wrap a piece of sandpaper. The second piece is now placed on the sandpaper and held in position by two brads. When the sandpaper is worn, the top piece of wood is removed, the worn piece of sandpaper replaced and the strip of wood tacked on as before.

Half-round Files: Saw ½″ dowel rods into halves lengthwise. Pass to each pupil a piece 7″ long. Saw and sandpaper a strip of 3/16″x7″x½″ basswood. Sandpaper is wrapped around the dowel rod, and the thin strip of basswood is placed and tacked to the dowel rod, thus holding the sandpaper in place. Renew the sandpaper when necessary.

How to Use the File

The saw does not leave the edges of the work very smooth. It is necessary therefore, to file them smooth. Do not file straight across the edge, but diagonally across, at the same time moving the file forward and away from the body. The flat file just constructed is used on the flat surfaces and convex curves. The half round file is used on hollow places,—that is, concave curves.

Sandpaper: How to Use It

After the sawing and filing are done, the work must be thoroughly cleaned by sandpapering it. A convenient way to do this is to wrap a small piece of sandpaper around a block of wood and rub the surface of the work with it. Sandpaper in the direction of the grain of the wood. Never sandpaper across the grain. All pencil and finger marks should be sandpapered away. To sandpaper the edges, place the sandpaper on a smooth surface and draw the wood over it. This aids in squaring up the edges.

To Finish String Winder

The soft surface of wood is very easily soiled and becomes discolored very quickly unless covered in some way with a protective coating like paint, varnish, shellac, or one of the numerous other finishes on the market. As paint spoils the beautiful appearance of the natural wood, it will not be considered. Varnish is not suitable for the work because great skill is necessary to properly apply it. To give a hard surface to the work, it should be given a coating of white shellac. It is more desirable to apply several coats of thin shellac to obtain the desired finish, than to attempt to secure that finish by applying one thick coat. After each application of shellac, the roughness should be removed by using worn sandpaper. For smoothing the edges, use the sandpaper file. To give the final polish, use a small amount of floor wax.

A dark color may be secured by using a solution of wood dye or stain. If this is done, the shellac should be applied after the coloring is dry. Any good wood stain may be used.

Match Scratch

Fig. 12, Plate 7, shows the constructive drawing for a match scratch. First draw the rectangle 3″x3¼″, as indicated by the dotted lines. Bisect the upper and lower edges as shown at "a" and "b." Place dots on the right and left edges, ⅝″ from the upper corners, as shown at "c" and "d." Connect these dots by continuous straight lines with the point "a" and by straight lines with the point "b."

With the straight line "cb" as a base, draw the arcs which intersect at "d." With this point of intersection as a center, draw the arc "cb." With the straight line "bd" as a base, draw the arcs which intersect at "c." With this point of intersection as a center, draw the arc "bd."

It will be remembered that this is simply an exercise based on the construction of equilateral triangles. Transfer the finished drawing to the wood as shown in Fig. 13. Fig. 14 shows the finished match scratch with sandpaper added.

To cut the sandpaper proceed to make the drawing the same as the drawing for the wood part, only make it smaller.

Pencil Sharpener

Fig. 15 shows a constructive drawing of a simple pencil sharpener.

First, draw a rectangle 4¼″x1″, as indicated by the dotted lines. Bisect the upper and lower edges. At each side of the point of bisection on the lower edge, place dots ¼″ from the center point. Connect these points with the corners above, as shown by the continuous straight lines. By using each point of bisection as a center, draw the arcs shown in Fig. 15.

Fig. 16 shows the drawing without the construction lines.

Fig. 17 shows the addition of the sandpaper.

It is quite possible for the teacher to work out a constructive drawing exercise for almost every problem which follows. By so doing, the work is divided between the drawing and the sawing.

The drawings contained in the outline are not to be passed to the pupils, but are only for the teacher's use.

It is very desirable that the pupils make their own drawings. If, however, any drawing contained in the outline is to be duplicated, this should be done by the teacher.

Transferring the Pattern to the Wood

The first step in transferring the pattern is to lay a piece of tracing material, such as tracing paper or tracing cloth, over the pattern shown in the plate. Now with a soft, sharp lead pencil trace the pattern on the tracing material. Select a piece of strawboard, cardboard or clothboard, place a piece of carbon paper face down on it, and then place the tracing material, on which the pattern is traced, over the carbon paper. Now by retracing the pattern on the tracing material it will be transferred, by means of the carbon paper, to the cardboard. With a sharp knife cut the pattern out of the cardboard. This cardboard pattern may now be laid on the wood and easily outlined. The original tracing should be preserved so that, if the cardboard pattern is lost, new ones may be made with very little effort.

Fig. 18 gives the pattern for a string winder, somewhat different in design from the one already made.

Figs. 19, 20 and 21 show three interesting and artistic pencil sharpeners. Here a little applied design is used in simple borders.

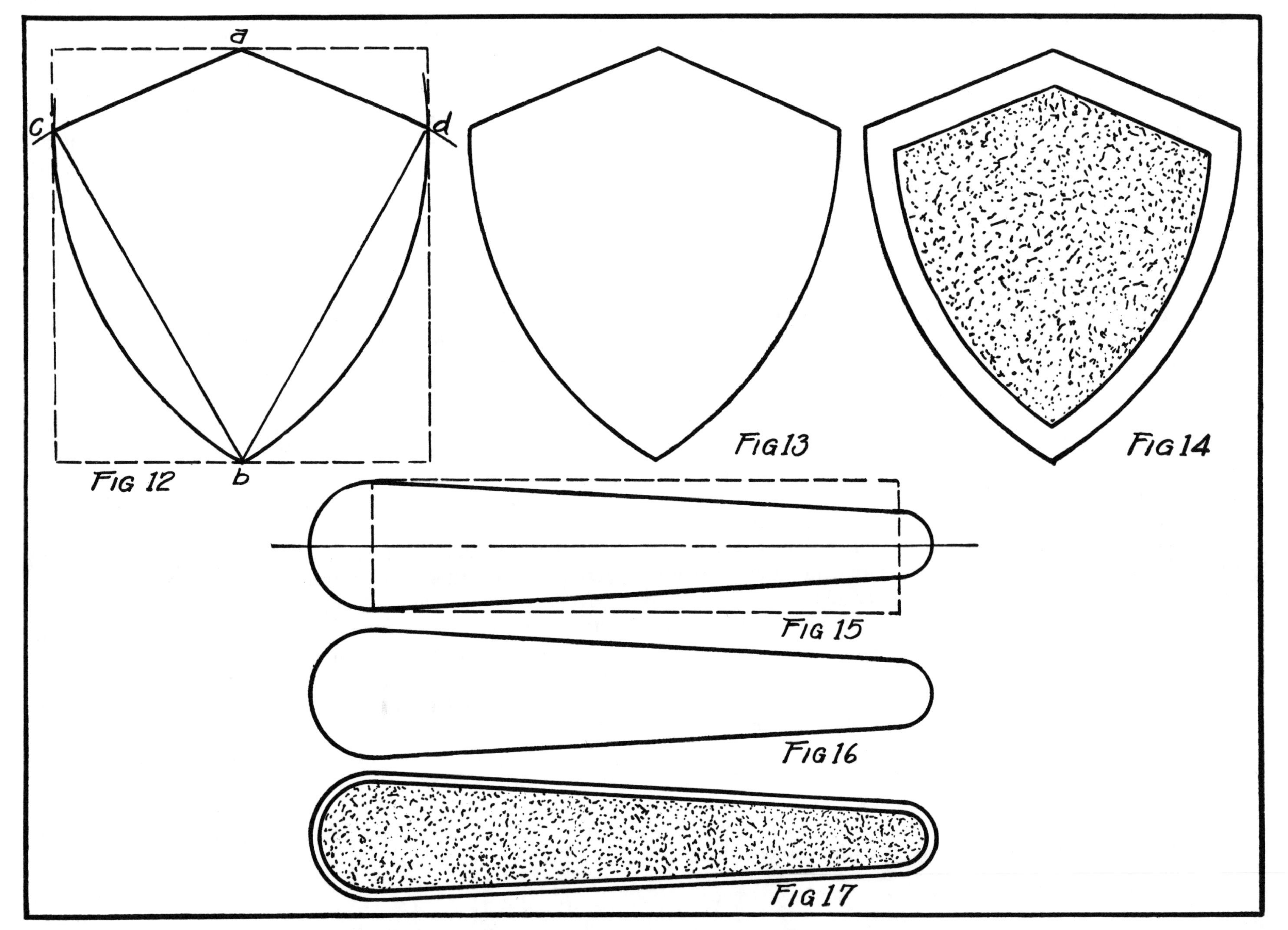

Plate 7—Development of Patterns for Match Scratch and Pencil Sharpener.

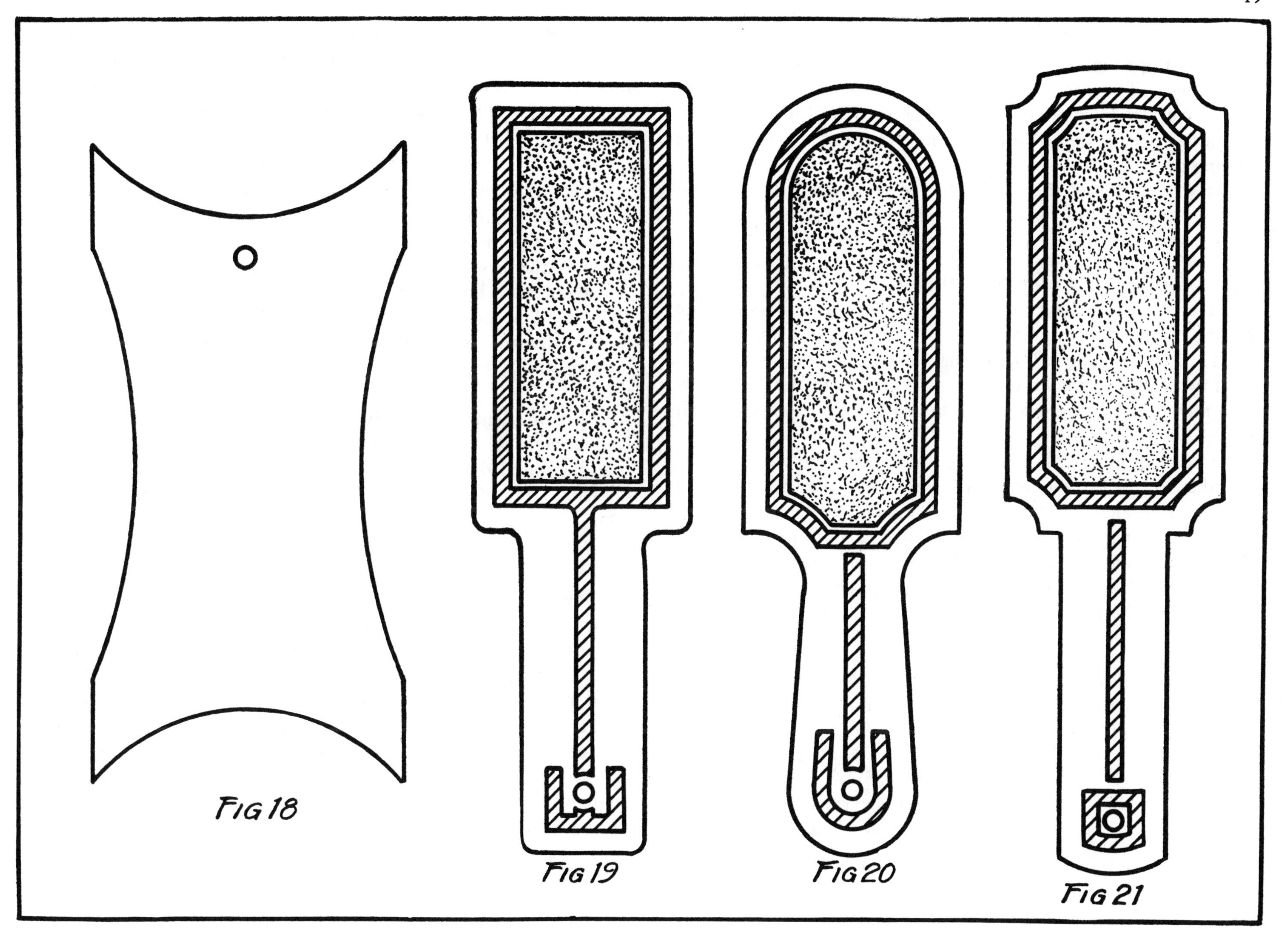

Plate 8—Patterns for String Winder and Pencil Sharpener.

SQUARED PAPER

By using squared paper the designing of toys is somewhat simplified. The drawings in Plate 9 show what fourth grade pupils can do on squared paper. The drawings may be transferred, as already described, from the paper to the wood and the sawing done.

It will be found that toys made in this way will not stand without a support of some kind. The completed figures of the soldier and boxer, in Plate 26, show a very simple standard.

COLORING OF TOYS

After the toys have been sawed and well finished in the natural wood, color may be applied. This may be done in two ways: First, regular oil paints may be used, giving the wood at least two coats. When thoroughly dry, a coat of shellac or varnish may be applied, thus giving the completed toy a very high gloss.

Second, the dry colors may be mixed with the white shellac and then applied to the toy. In this way the color and gloss are produced in one process.

By mixing the color with the shellac, a mixture is obtained that resembles the enamels furnished by various paint companies.

In Plate 10 are found a few flat forms that find a place in the work of the fourth grade.

PAPER KNIVES

The paper knives, shown in Plate 11, while in the flat, afford most excellent opportunities for simple design. Color may be applied, thus adding new interest.

TRELLISES

In Plate 12 are found drawings of several trellises, simple enough in construction for a fourth grade class.

These problems give the boys an opportunity to use brads and hammers. The trellis to the left is a good illustration of making long cuts with the coping-saw blade, placed in the side of the frame. The trellis should find a place in the window box or school garden.

RECTANGULAR TRAY

The rectangular pin tray shown in Plate 13 makes an interesting home problem and, when well constructed, finds a place on the dresser or sewing table.

It is the first problem in which the saw blade is passed through a small hole. This hole is drilled with an awl, shown in Plate 3. The saw blade is then passed through it and placed in the saw frame. This is done to saw away an inner rectangle, leaving a sort of picture frame which forms the rim of the tray.

This problem lends itself to simple decoration, which may be applied in oil or enamel to the rim·

The dotted lines in the drawing show the position in which the rim is placed on the smaller rectangle which forms the bottom.

DRAWING AN ELLIPSE

In Plate 14 is shown a very simple, yet very accurate, method of drawing an ellipse, when the long and short diameters are known. Set one point or leg of a compass or dividers on the center or intersection of the two diameters as at "d"; set the other point or leg at "e," the extreme end of the long diameter. The dividers are now set with a distance equal to one-half of the long diameter. Now set a point of the dividers at "c," the extreme end of the short diameter and with the other point strike arcs, cutting the long diameter at "a" and "b." Now place a pin, or small brad, in each point "a," "b" and "c." Take a piece of string and loop it around three pins or brads and tie it firmly

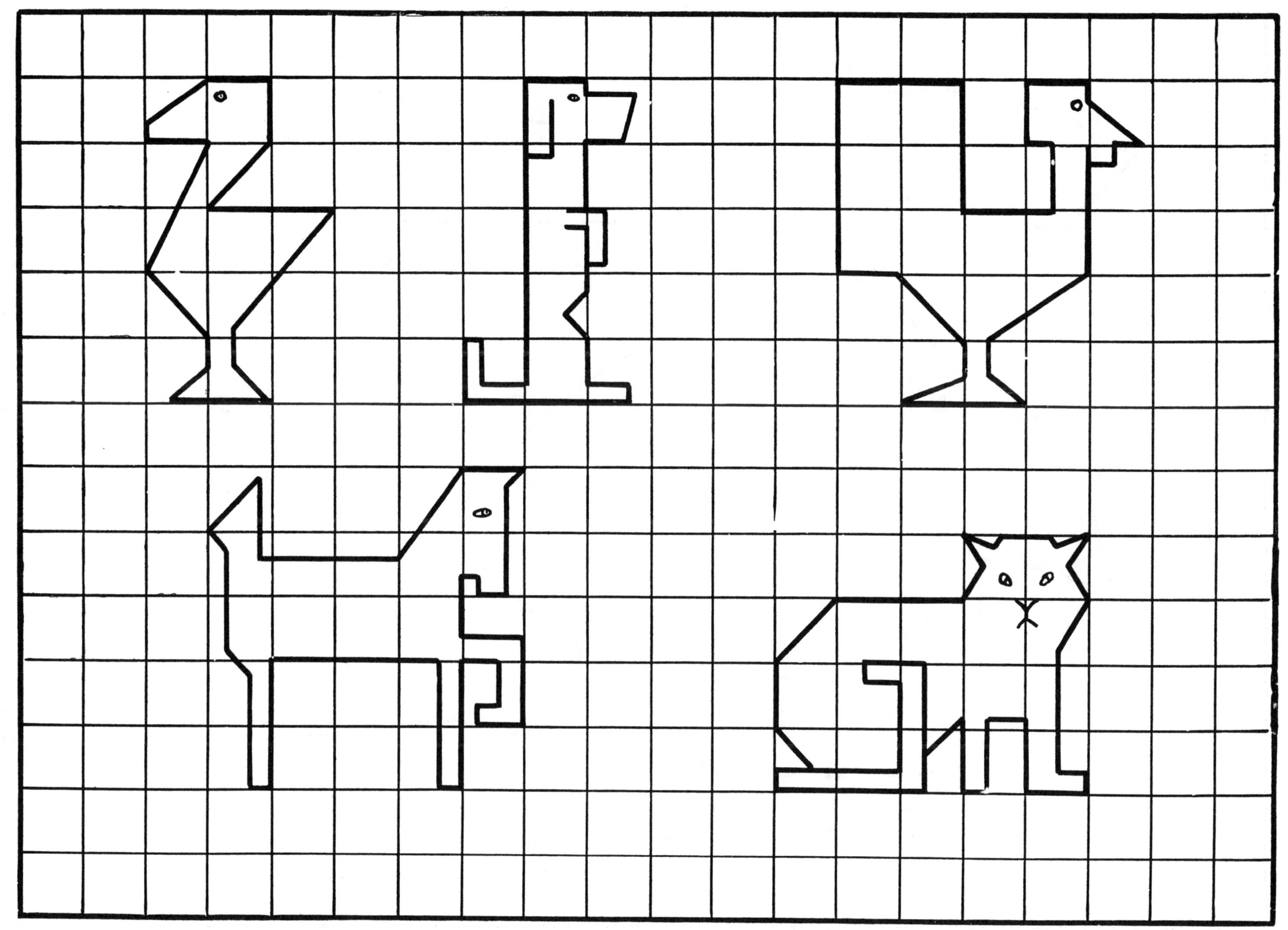

Plate 9—Method of Using Squared Paper to Obtain Patterns for Simple Objects.

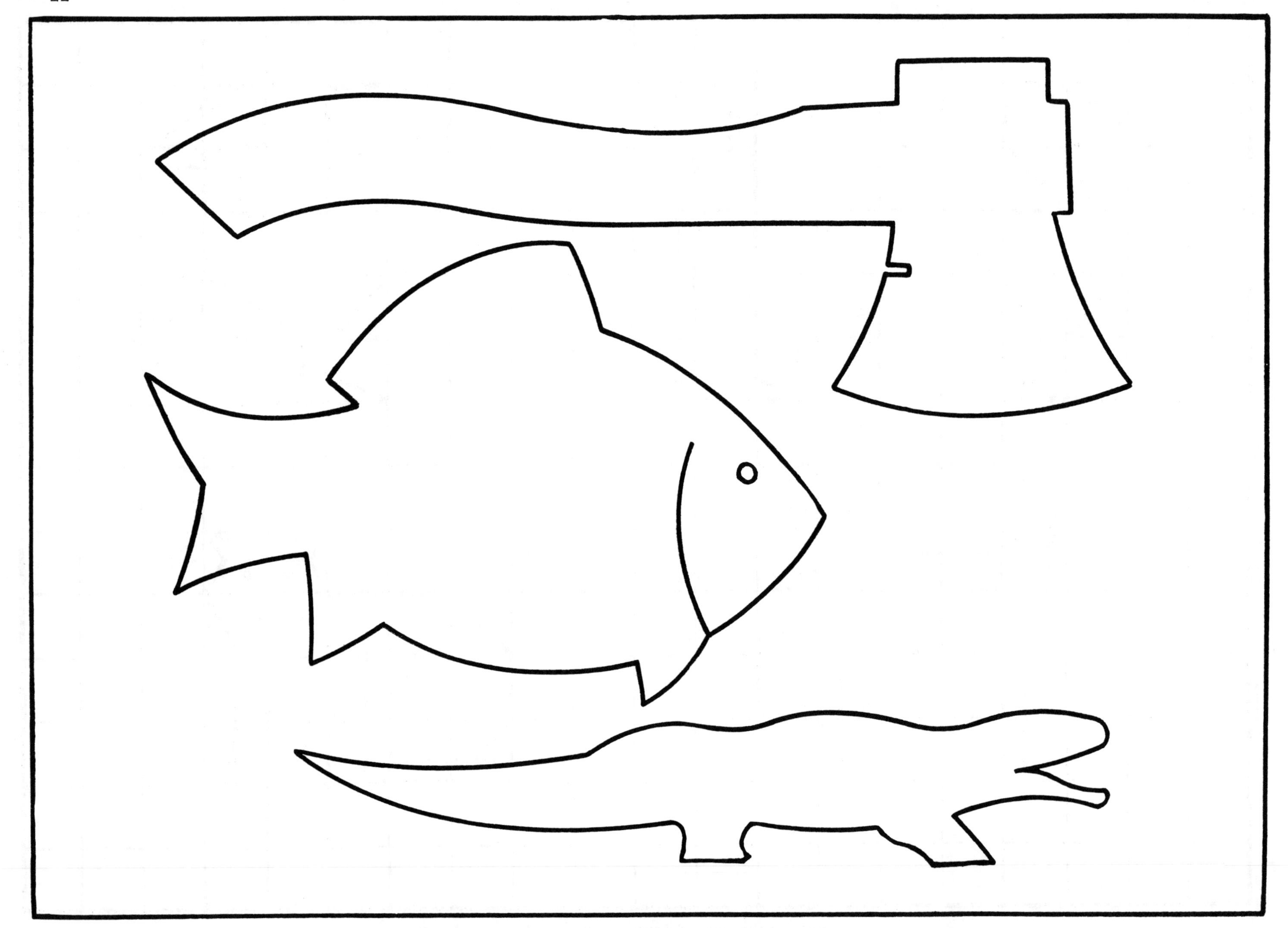

Plate 10—Patterns for Simple One-piece Flat Work.

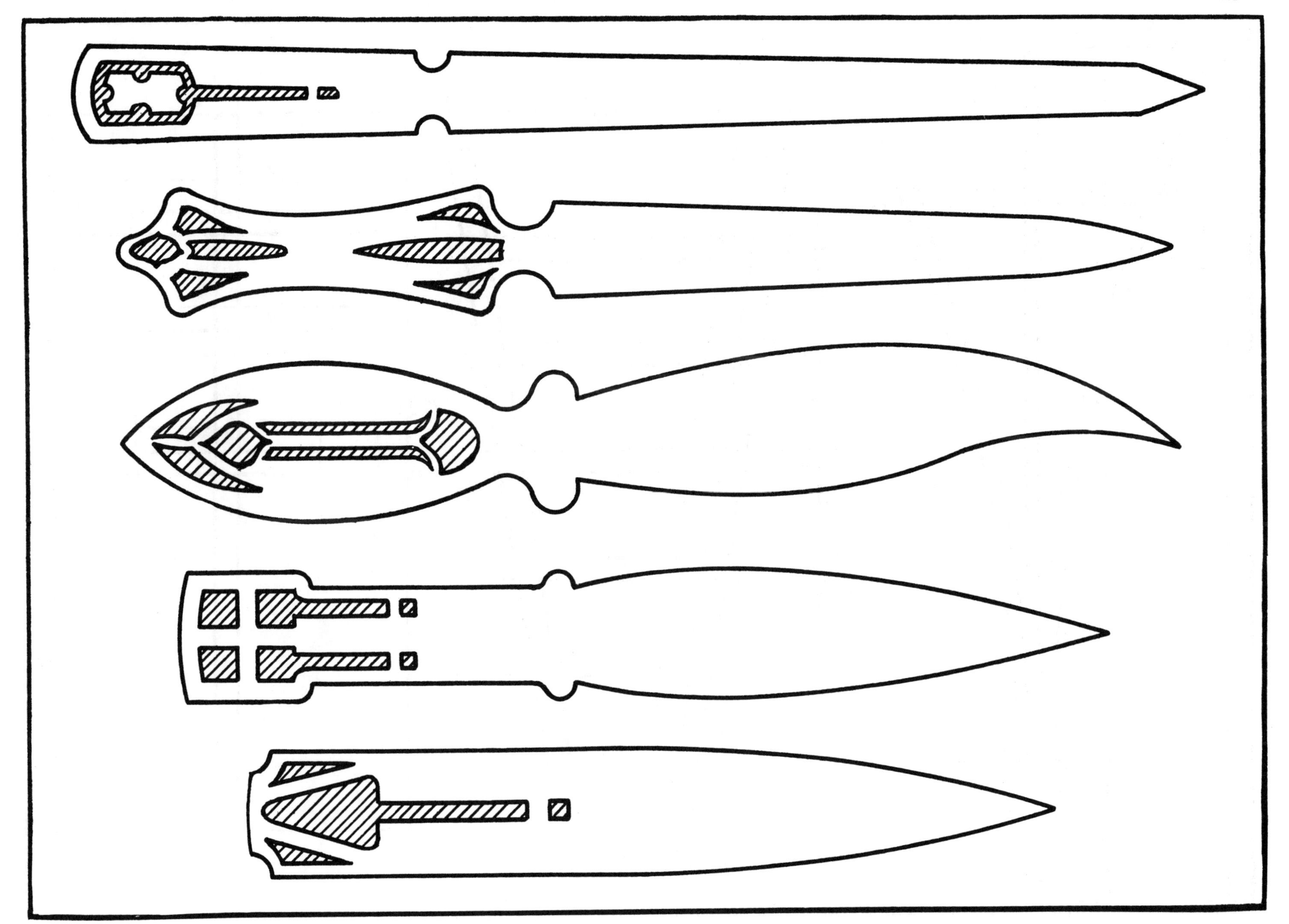

Plate 11—Patterns and Designs for Paper Knives.

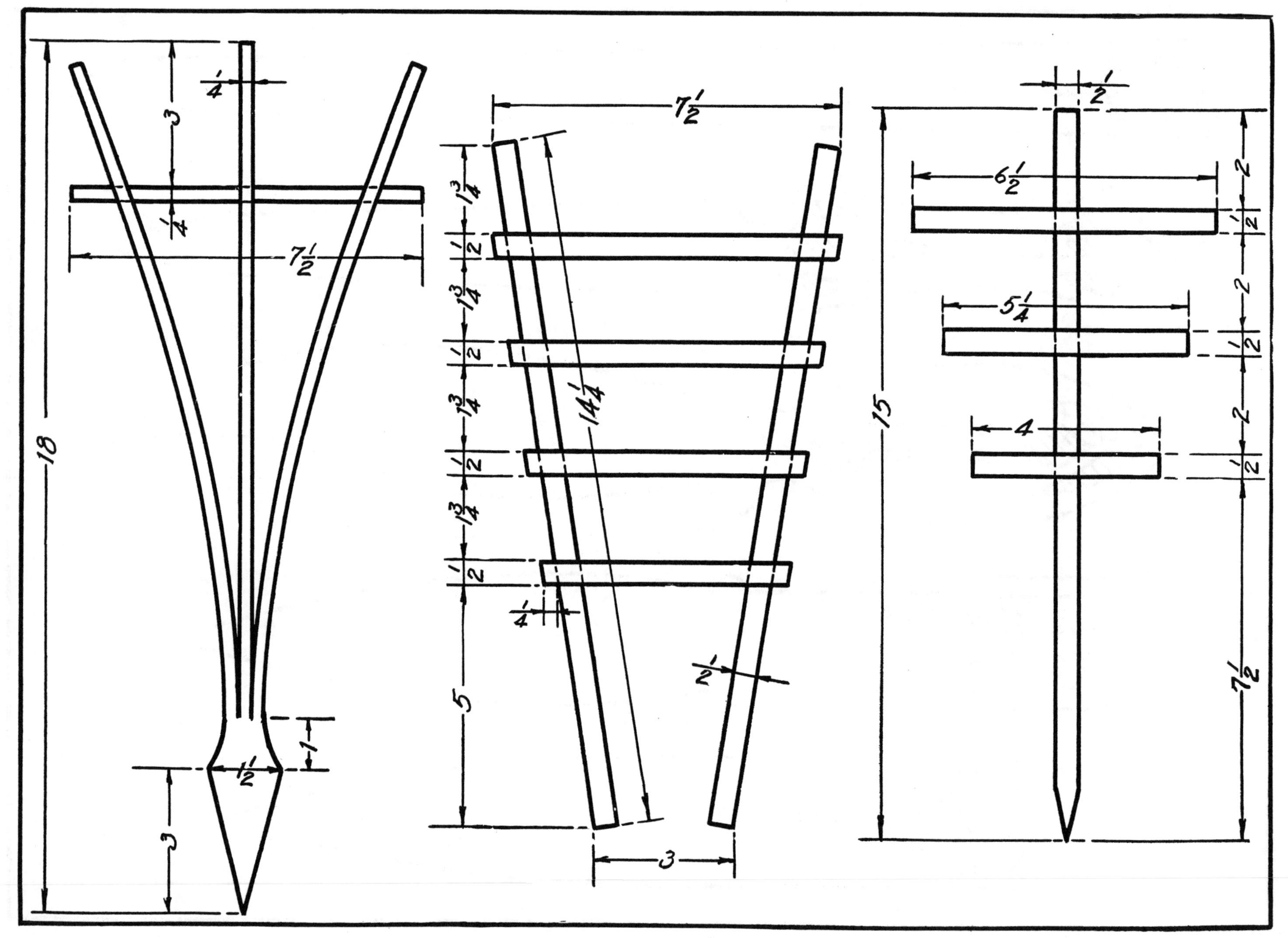

Plate 12—Drawings for Trellises.

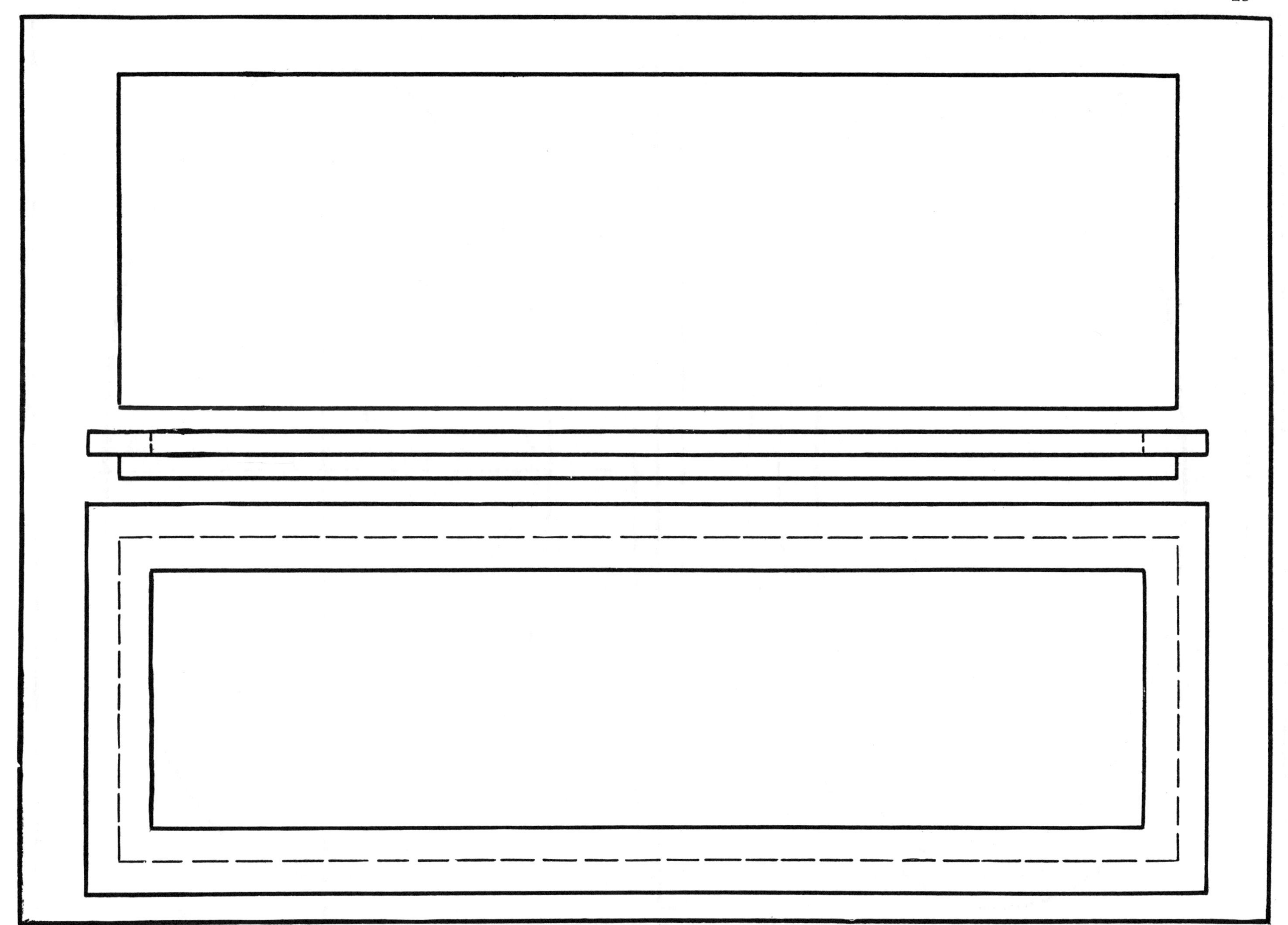

Plate 13—Pattern for Rectangular Pin Tray.

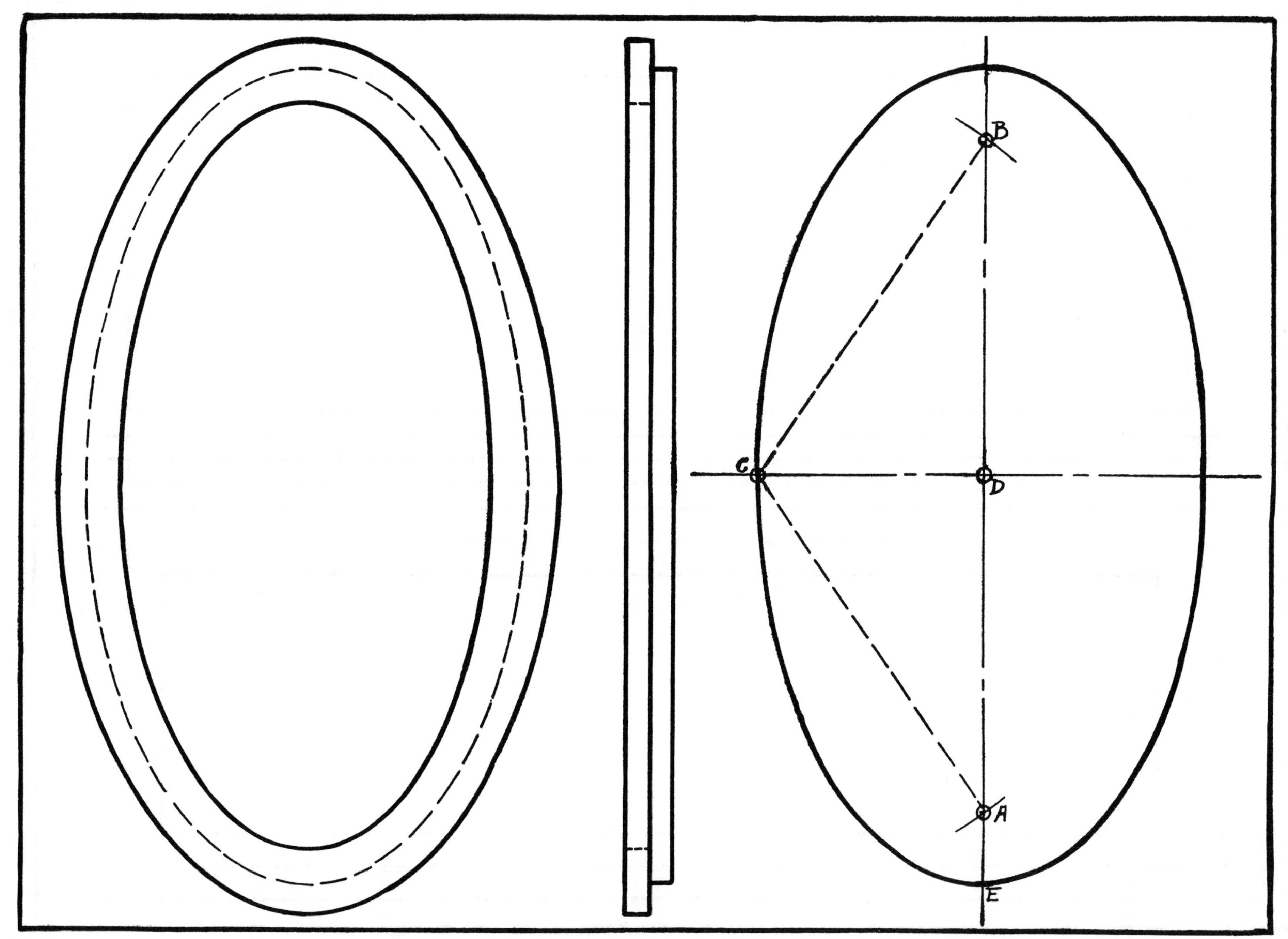

Plate 14—Pattern for Elliptical Pin Tray with Method of Drawing an Ellipse.

with a hard knot. Remove the pin at "c," put the point of a pencil in its place, and keeping an even tension on the string with the point of the pencil, move the pencil outward and around, and a true ellipse will be traced.

To give the pupils practice in the drawing and cutting of ellipses, an elliptical-shaped tray can be constructed, as shown in Plate 14, the pupils making the drawings rather than tracing the patterns. The tray consists of a flat, solid ellipse, made of light wood, and a flat, elliptical band ½ inch wide, which is tacked to the flat ellipse.

The tray can be made attractive by placing a simple design around the ½ inch band. Care should be taken, when sawing out the band, to see that the work is held firmly against the sawing board, otherwise it is likely to split.

BIRD STICKS

Plate 15 shows five interesting patterns for bird shapes to be placed on bird sticks. These patterns should be transferred to light wood and very carefully sawed out. After they are sawed, the edges of the shapes should be well filed and the entire pieces sandpapered. They may then be colored as indicated in the plate, either with oil colors or white shellac colored with dry colors. Long, thin sticks or dowel rods should be cut and fastened to the branches on which the birds are sitting. These may be made of the light basswood. Small twigs of trees also may be used with artistic effects. The children may be led to draw some original bird shapes to cut out and color.

ONE-PIECE TOYS

Each of the following 22 toys is considered a one-piece problem and is planned especially for beginners. Toys of this type may be cut from basswood or poplar wood, ½ inch in thickness. One-piece toys may be made more interesting by attaching wheels to the platforms on which they stand.

A 1 inch or 1¼ inch dowel rod, cut into disks ¼ inch in thickness, makes very good wheels. Axles may be made of 3/16 inch dowel rods, and the wheels can be kept in place with ½ inch or ¾ inch cotter pins driven through the axles. A small nail will also make a satisfactory axle.

MAKING A STENCIL

All drawings of animals and other projects in this manual have been made full size, so that teachers and pupils will not be obliged to enlarge the drawings.

The coloring of animal features, etc., on toys often becomes quite a task. To simplify the process and to insure uniformly satisfactory results, the stencil has been found very helpful.

To make a stencil, place a piece of carbon paper, with the black side down, on the paper to which the design is to be transferred. Then, place the drawing on the carbon paper and trace the outline. When the design has been satisfactorily copied on the stencil paper, cut away all the colored spots, leaving openings in place of them. It is well to make the stencil of rather heavy, stiff paper.

The cut-out drawing or stencil, as it is properly called, may be placed on the toy and the inner edges of each opening may be traced with a pencil.

Stencils once cut may be used many times, thus very greatly simplifying the work of the teacher.

JOINTED FORMS

Thus far, we have dealt only with flat, simple toys. We come now to toys which are made of several pieces joined together with movable joints. Plate 38 shows a Jester and Horse which is made up of a number of pieces, loosely joined by means of cotter pins and rivet burrs.

Cotter pins or split pins, as they are sometimes called, resemble small brads except that they are split instead of being

Plate 15—Patterns and Color Chart for Bird Sticks.

Plate 16—Pattern for Crow.

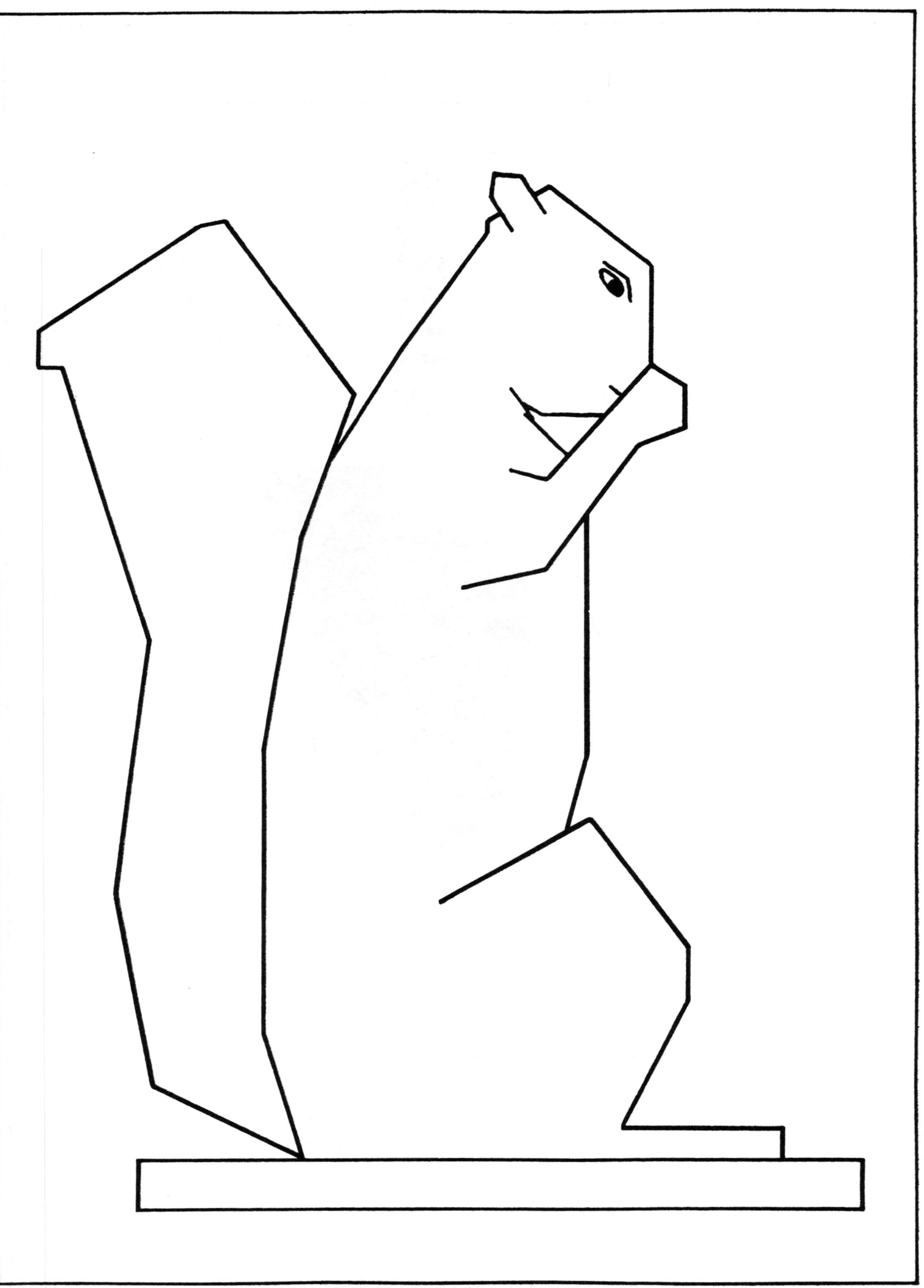

Plate 17—Pattern for Squirrel.

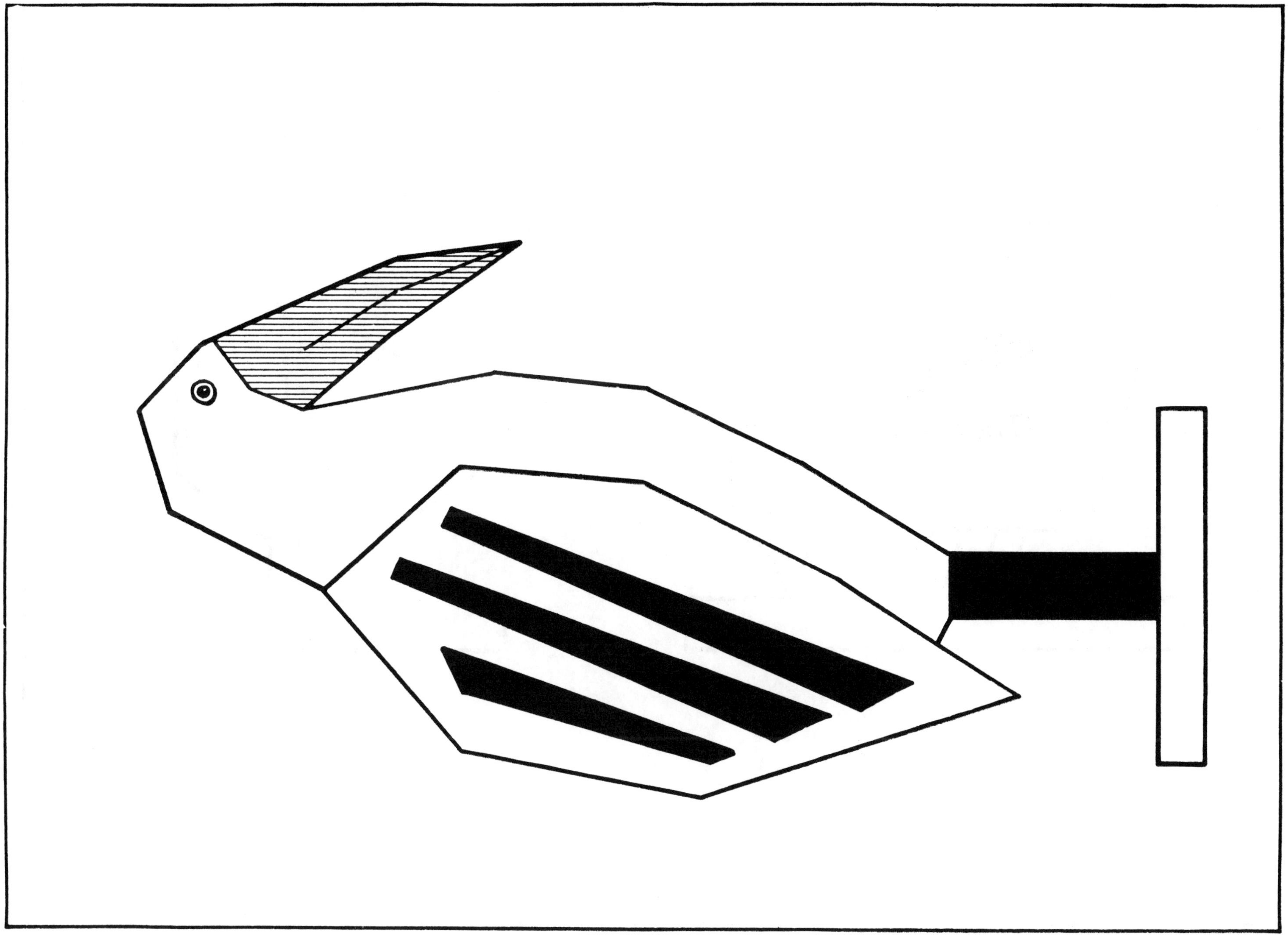

Plate 18—Pattern for Pelican.

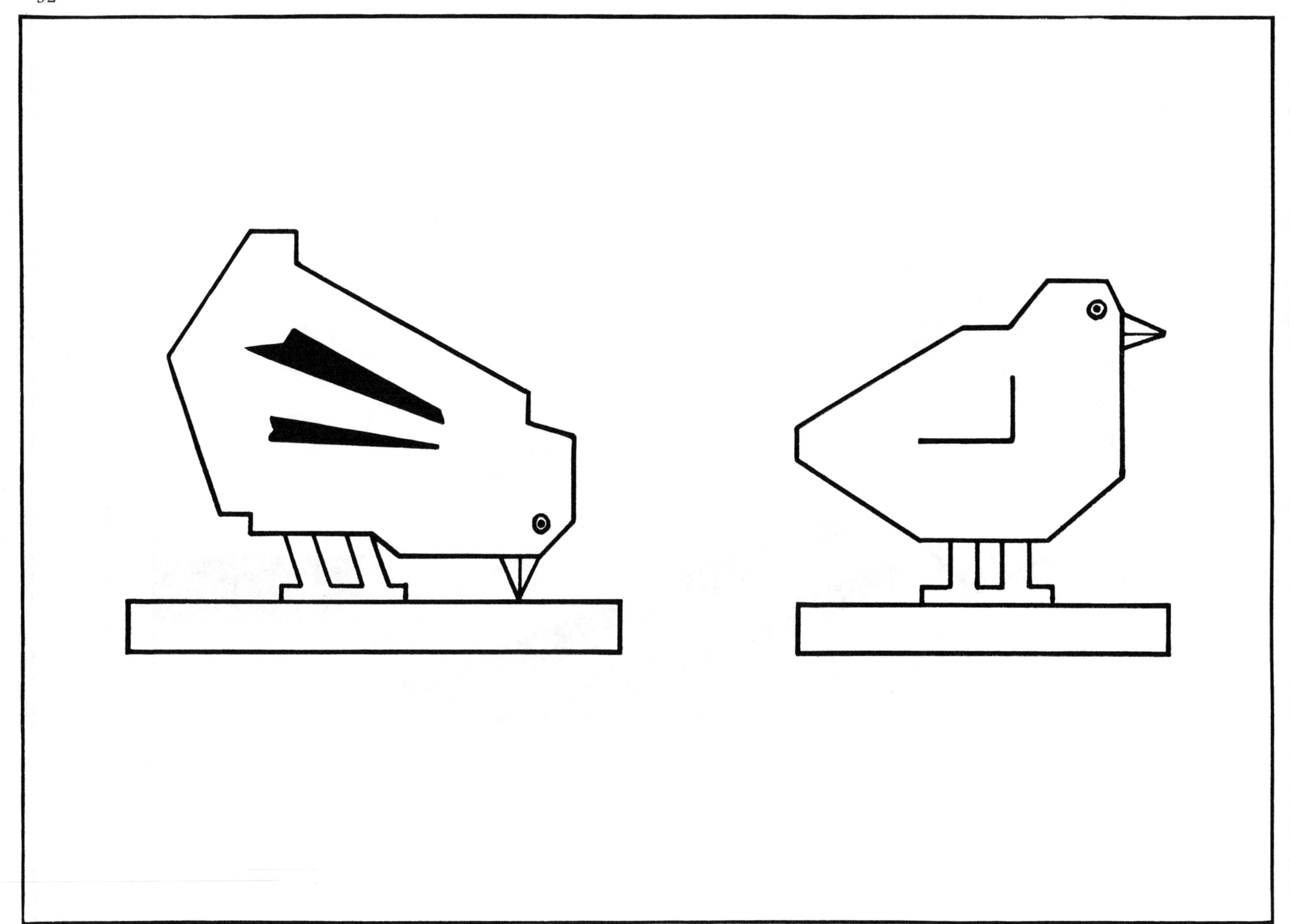

Plate 19—Pattern for chicks.

Plate 20—Pattern for Dog.

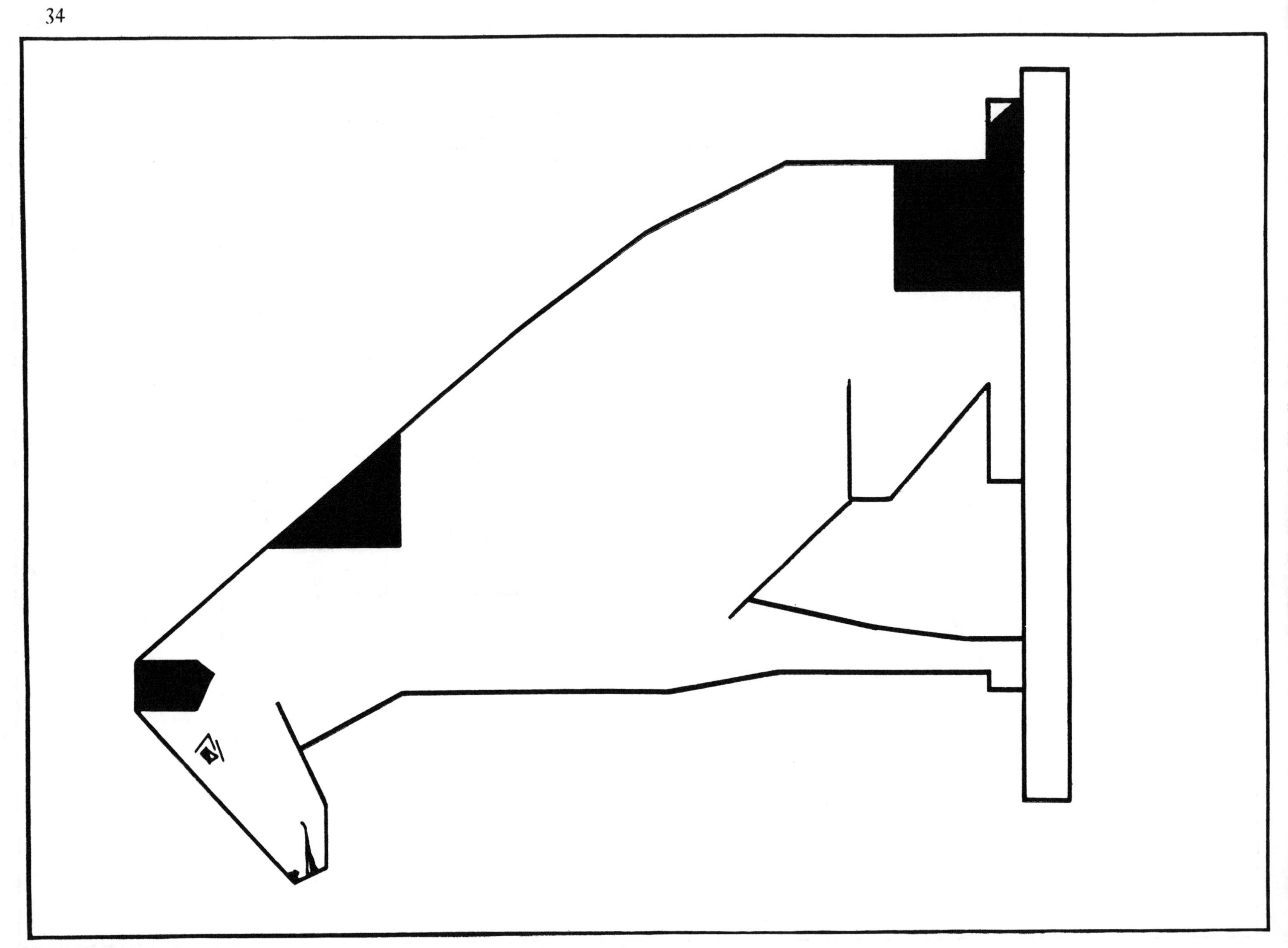

Plate 22—Pattern for Bear.

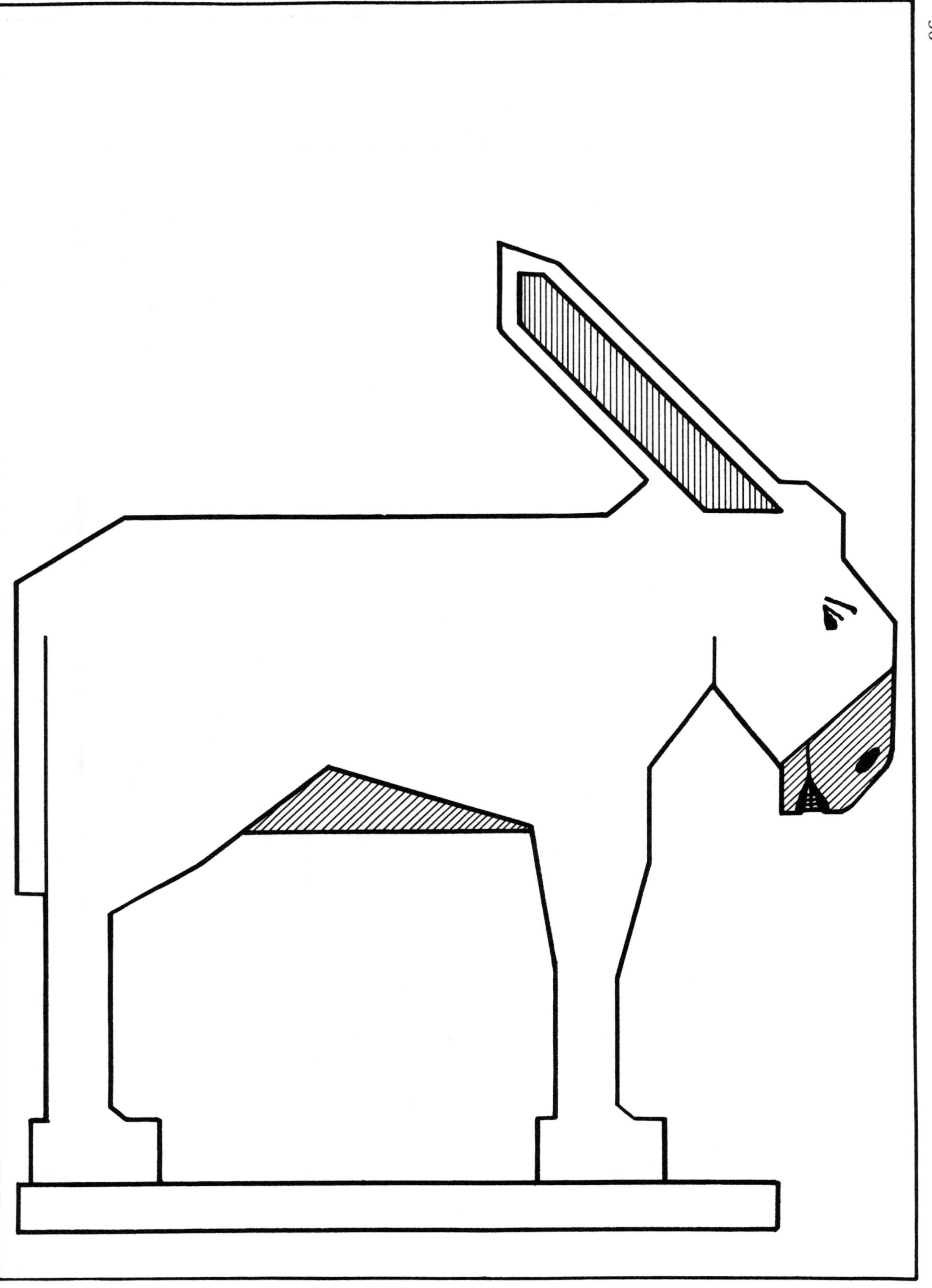

Plate 23—Pattern for Donkey.

Plate 24—Pattern for Lion.

Plate 25—Pattern for Cow.

Plate 26—Pattern for Camel.

Plate 27—Pattern for Goat.

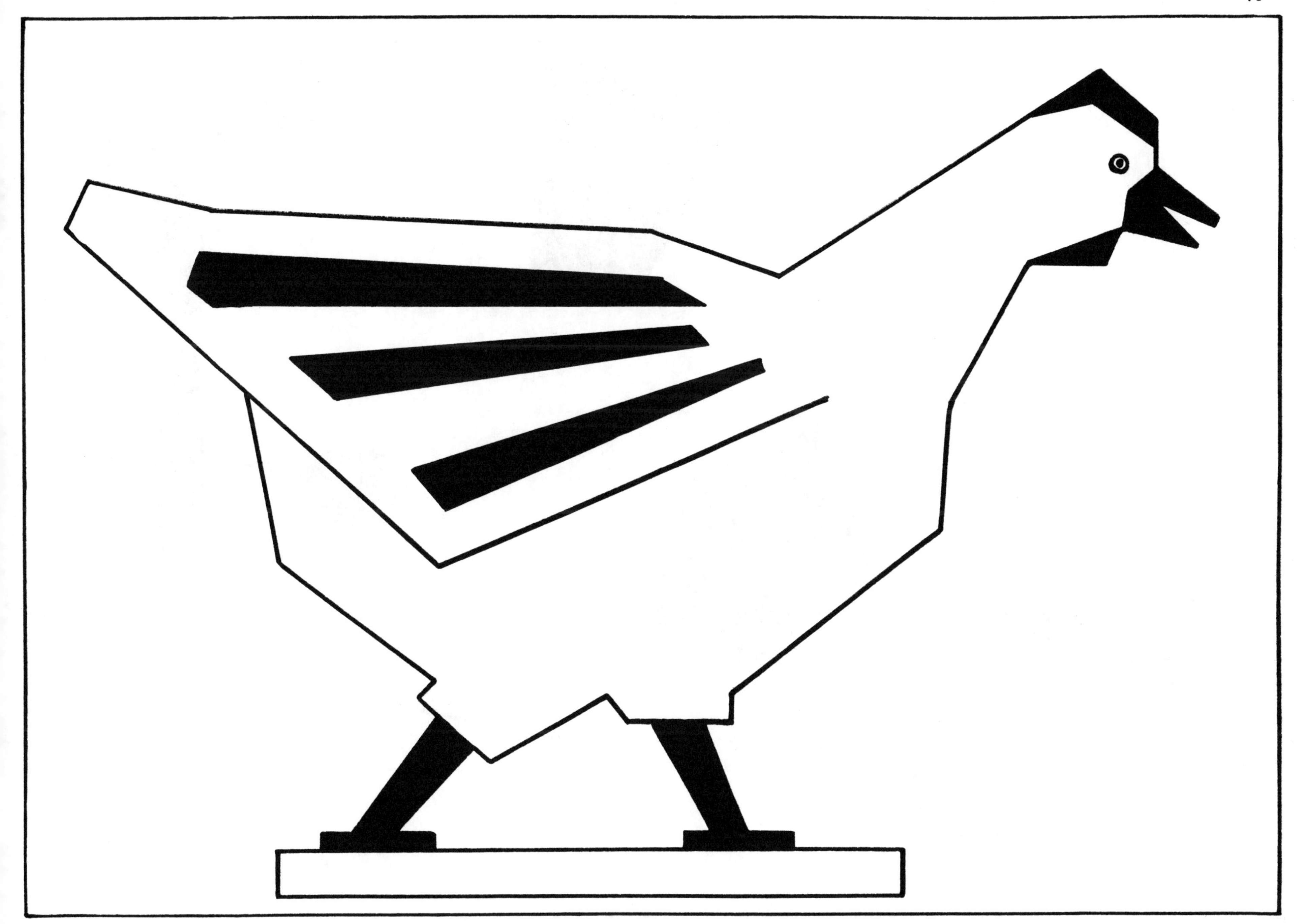

Plate 28—Pattern for Hen.

Plate 29—Pattern for Cat.

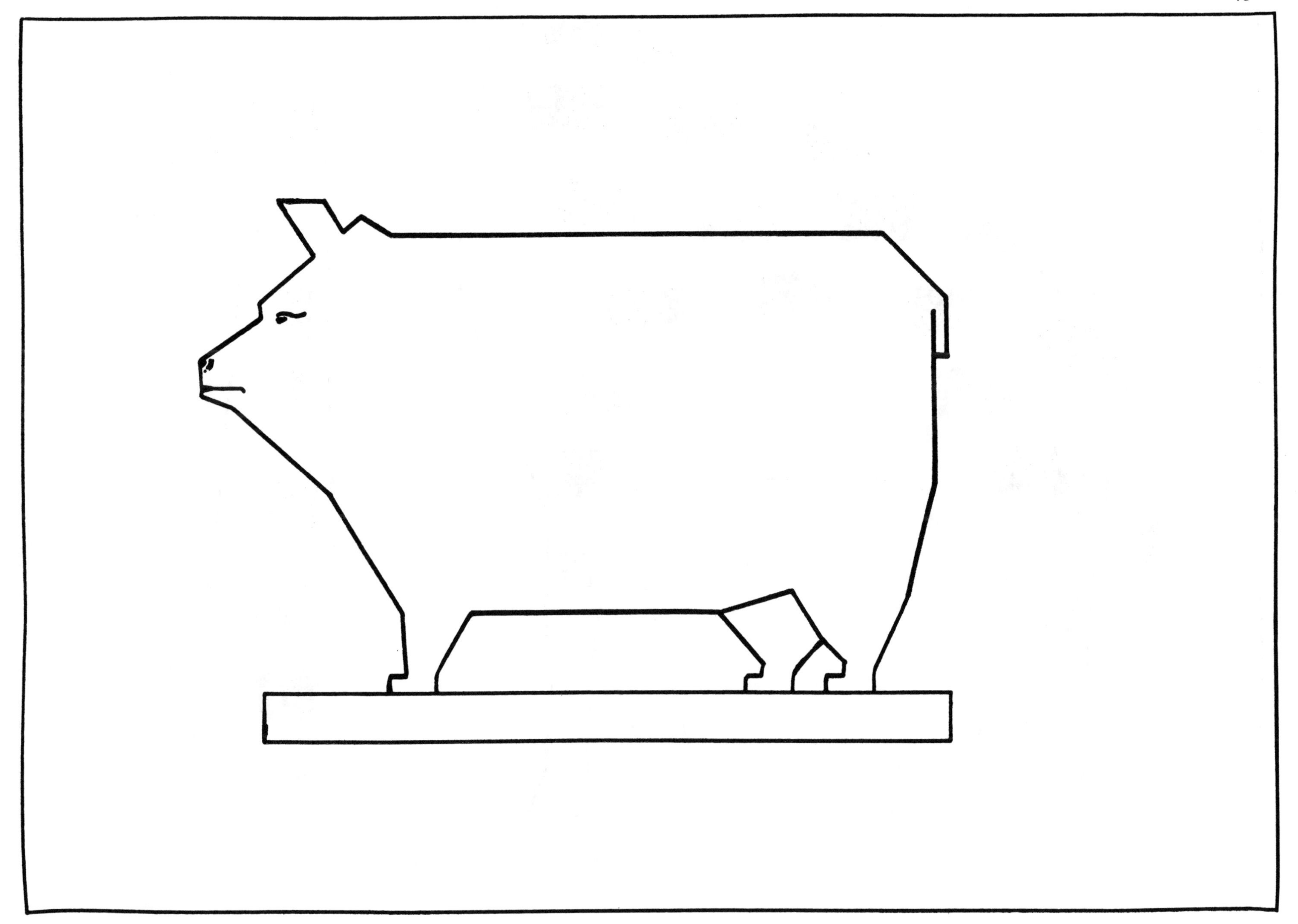

Plate 30—Pattern for Pig.

Plate 31—Pattern for Giraffe.

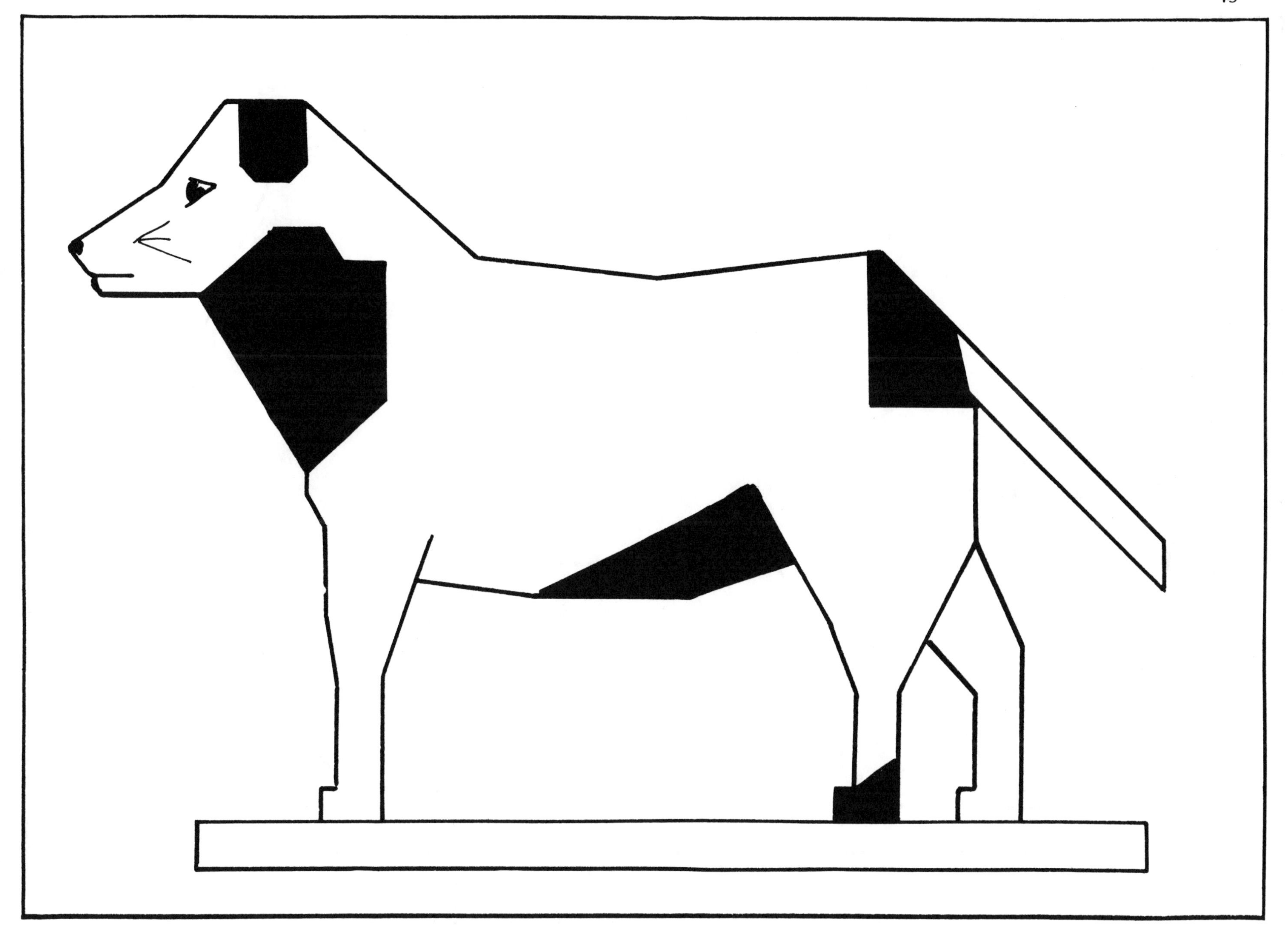

Plate 32—Pattern for Dog.

Plate 33—Pattern for Elephant.

Plate 34—Pattern for Rabbit.

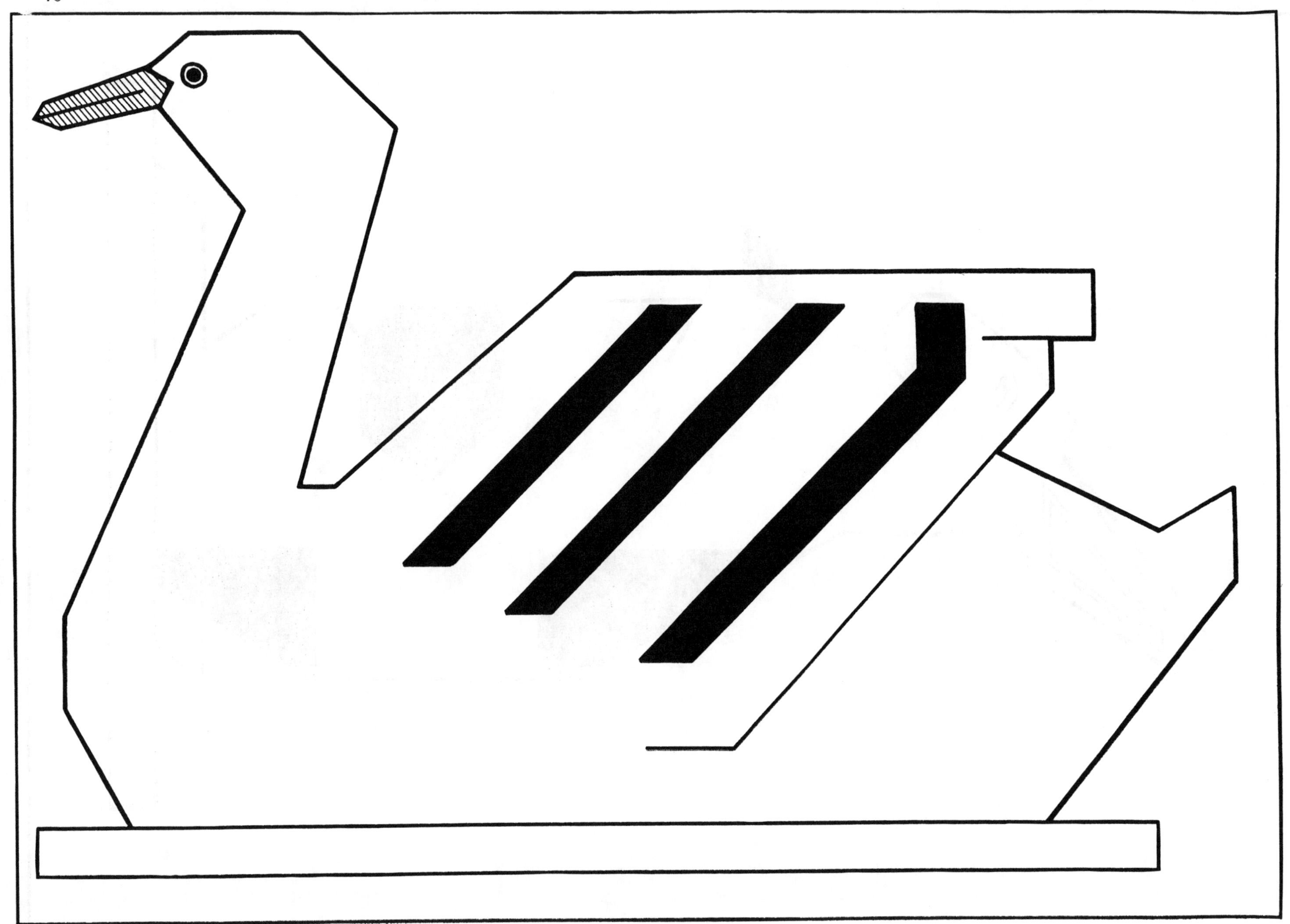

Plate 35—Pattern for Swan.

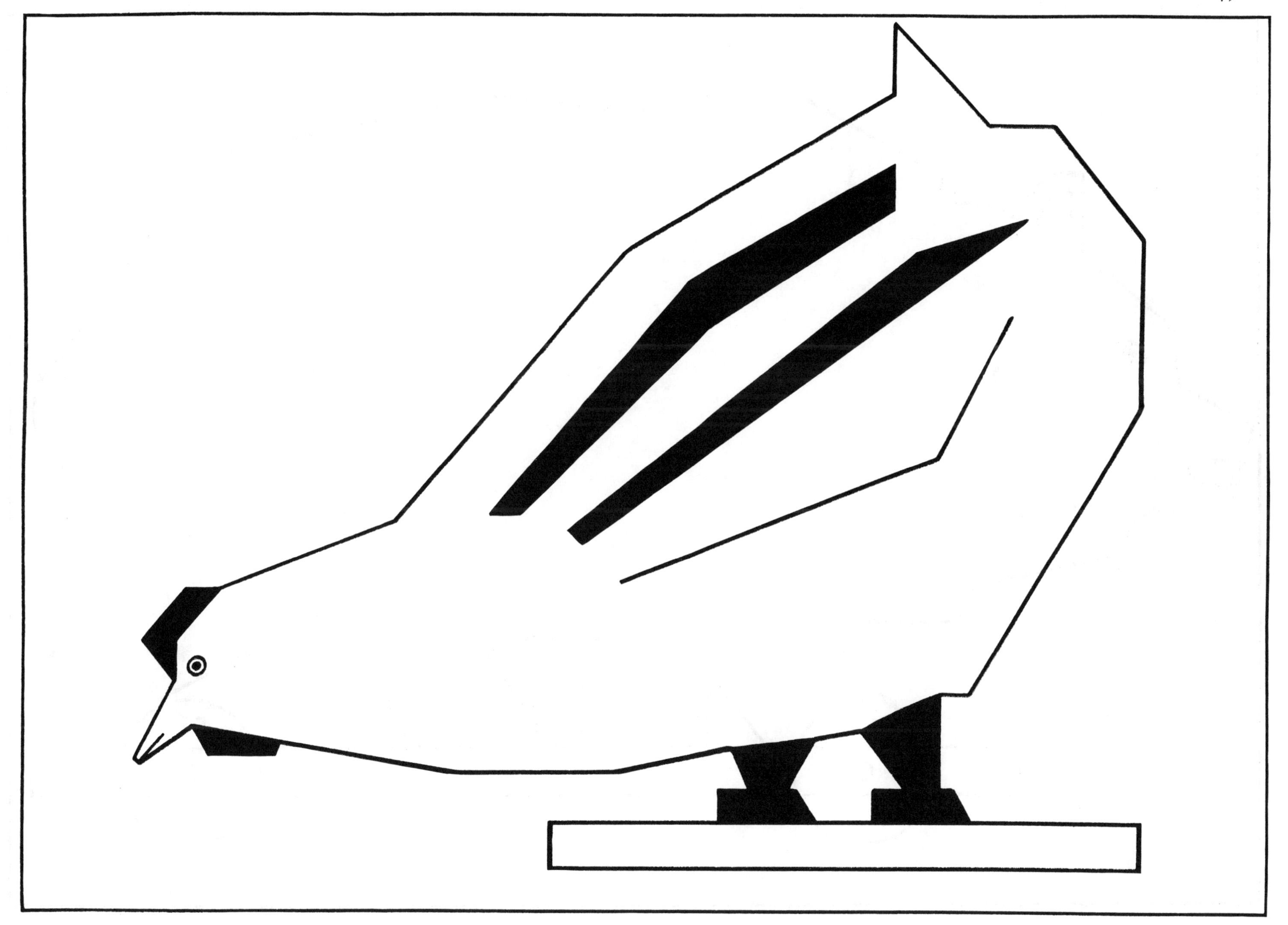

Plate 36—Pattern for Feeding Hen.

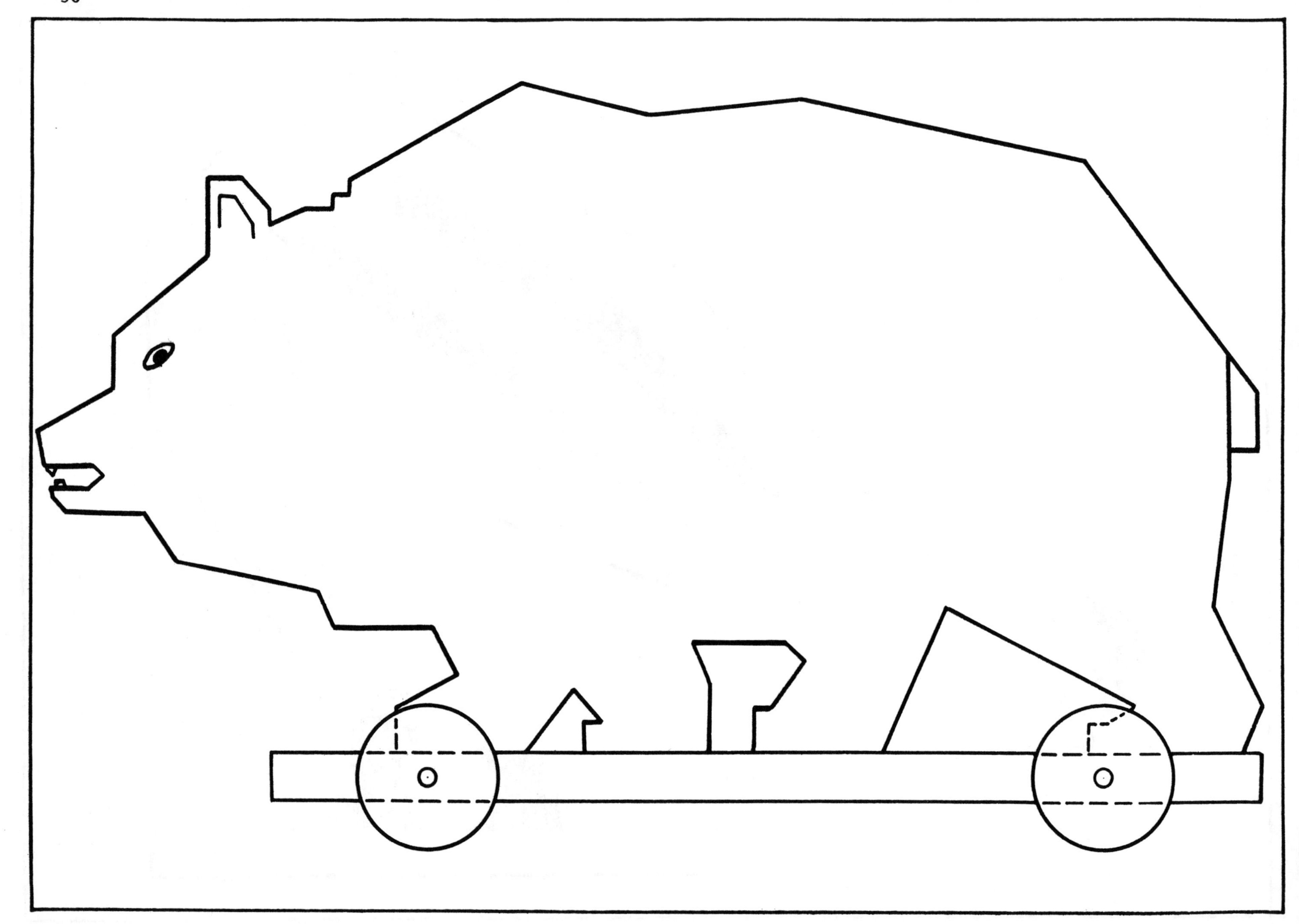

Plate 37—Pattern for Bear on Wheels.

solid, and have a loop instead of a solid head. After holes are bored in a toy with an awl, cotter pins may be put through several pieces which are to be joined, and the split ends of the pins may be bent away from each other, as shown in the sketch in the upper right-hand corner of Plate 3. This fastens the pieces together loosely, yet very securely. The cotter pins can be removed and replaced, loosened or tightened, with very little or no trouble. Small rivet burrs are used with the cotter pins, to act as washers. if cotter pins are too long for a given toy, they may be cut off with side-cutting pliers. They form a neat, substantial, and effective means of joining the different parts of a toy.

Plate 39 shows the patterns for the several pieces that go to make up the finished Jester, shown in Plate 38. The dots enclosed by the small circles mark the places where the small holes are to be bored for the cotter pins, which are to hold the pieces together. The letters marking the small circles represent the holes that are to be placed together. For instance, the hole marked "A" on the head of the Jester must be placed behind the hole marked "A" on the body of the Jester.

The figures enclosed by the medium-size circles represent the required number of pieces of each pattern. In other words, where the figure 2 is seen enclosed by a circle, it means that two of this pattern are to be made. If no number is given, just one piece of that particular pattern is to be made. For instance, the total number of pieces required for the Jester is twelve, yet only seven patterns are shown.

The parts should be joined together very loosely. One end of a rubber string can be placed through a hole in the head and the other end tied to a rod. When the rod is moved, the Jester will bound up and down and, if loosely joined, the parts will gyrate freely.

Before joining the parts, they should be well sanded and then colored with bright, contrasting colors.

Plate 41 gives the pattern for the different parts which form the Horse, with the exception of the head shown in Plate 40. The Horse may be made to stand, by using a flat board with a slot cut in it, similar to the one used for the Soldier and the Ball Player shown in Plate 52. Or the Horse may be tacked to a rolling stand, such as is used with the animals in Plate 43.

JOINTED ANIMALS ON MOVABLE STANDS

Plate 43 shows a number of jointed animals made up of flat wood and mounted on movable stands or carts. These make very interesting toys for small children, as they can be pulled around like wagons or carts.

Plate 44 shows two forms of movable stands commonly used. They are very simple in construction. The wheels are ¼ inch or ⅜ inch sections of 1 inch dowel rods, as shown in Plate 3. Common nails or 1 inch brads may be used as axles. The method used to attach an animal toy to a stand depends upon the construction of the animal. If constructed like the Buffalo or Ostrich, shown in Plate 43, the stand is made like the one shown in the upper half of Plate 44, in which the legs are tacked to the outside of a single strip placed down the center of the stand. If the toy is made like the Goose or Goat, shown in Plate 43, then the stand is constructed like the one in the lower half of Plate 44, in which two strips are tacked to the center of the stand to form a groove just the thickness of the wood of the animal. The legs or feet of the animal are forced into this groove. Very amusing results may be obtained by placing the nails, which form the axle, off center in the wheels. This will cause the stand and animal to bob up and down as it is run over the floor. A variety of stands or platforms may be constructed and different parts of the animals may be con-

Plate 38—Jester and Horse.

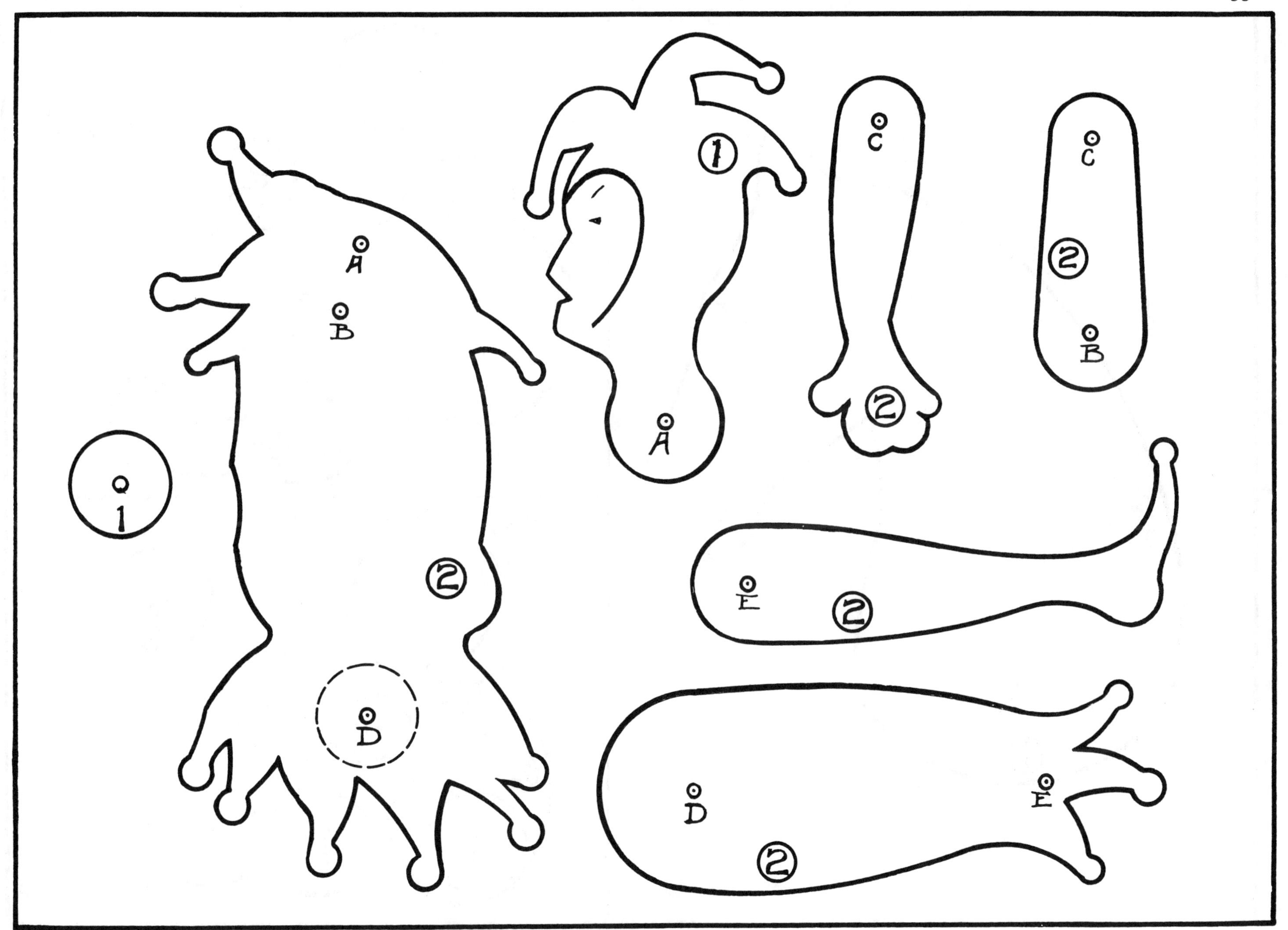

Plate 39—Patterns for Jester.

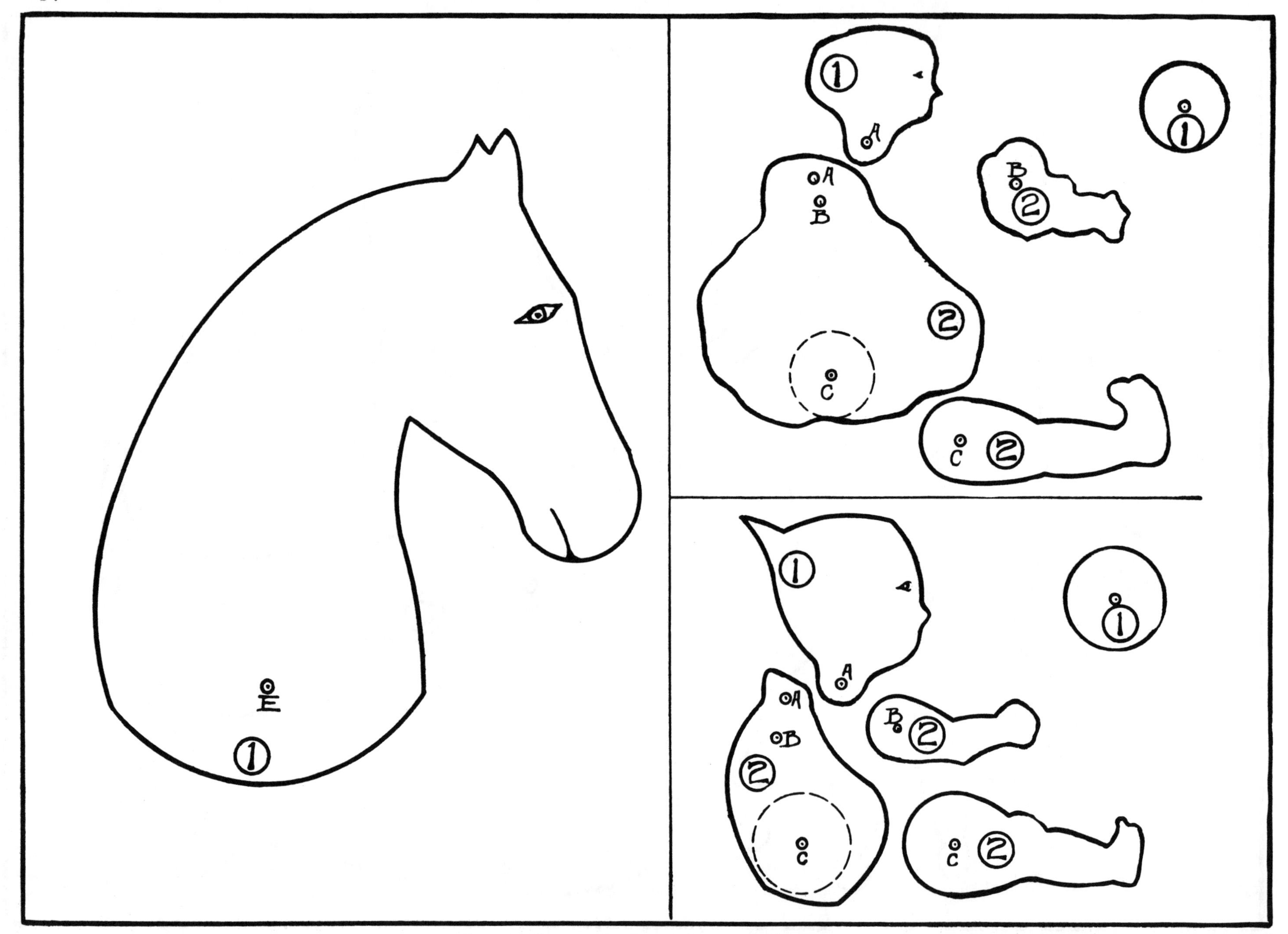

Plate 40—Patterns for Horse's Head and Kewpies.

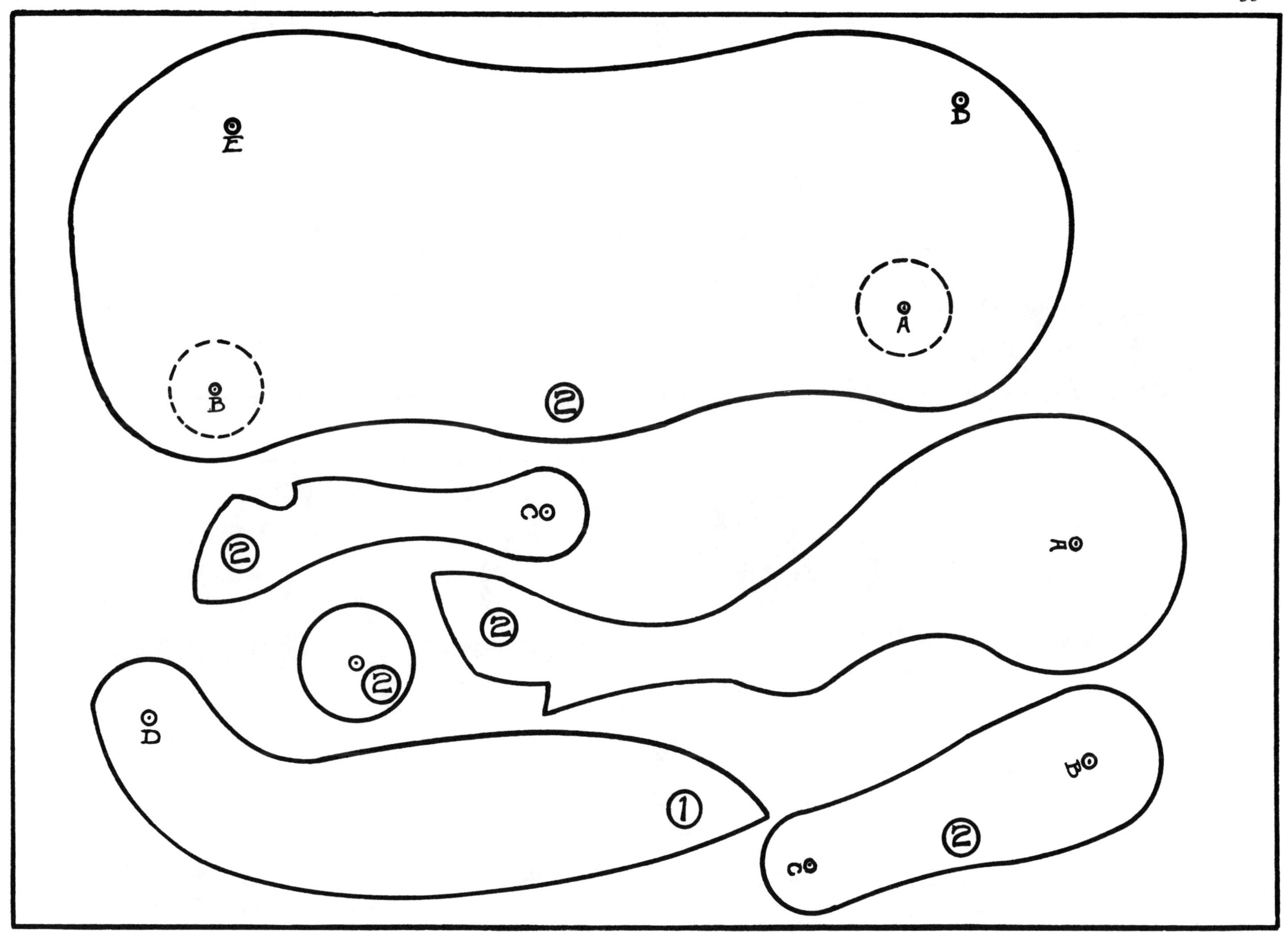

Plate 41—Patterns for Horse.

Plate 42—Jointed Animals.

Plate 43—Jointed Animals on Movable Stands.

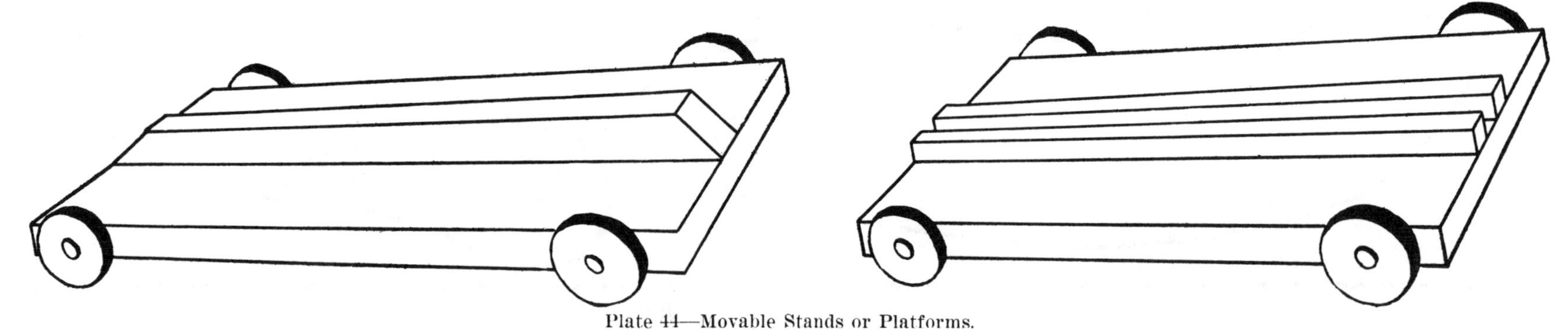

Plate 44—Movable Stands or Platforms.

nected with the wheels or axles of the stands, producing interesting variations and odd motions.

There are great possibilities in this interesting line of activity, giving a wide scope for ingenuity on the part of the teacher and the pupils. The teacher should arouse the interest of every child by designing and suggesting new and interesting types of toys.

The toys must be well finished and carefully colored to be appreciated. Discourage hasty, untidy work, for the habits which the child forms will remain with him in other work. Rather an effort should be made to see that the child forms only those habits that will be a benefit to him later in life.

MECHANICAL TOYS

Most children show greater interest in the construction of motion toys than in one-piece, stationary toys. The stationary toys are simpler and more easily made, and naturally precede those in which many parts are assembled to complete the whole.

Plate 59 shows the various parts necessary for the construction of a Jumping Jack, and Plate 60 shows the parts assembled. The moving parts are held together by burrs and cotter pins. If no other boring tool is at hand, the holes may be bored with a 1/16 inch brad awl. Where there are two holes, one is used for the cotter pin and the other for the string, which is so tied as to cause the parts to move when pulled. The various parts must be very loosely jointed, so that their weight will cause them to resume their original position after the string is released. The Jumping Jack when highly colored makes a most pleasing toy.

FEEDING HENS

Plate 61 shows the full size of the Feeding Hens toy. The slides which work the Hens are drawn one-half size. Plate 64 shows the Hens fastened to the slides. Here again the cotter pins are used as fasteners, the holes being large enough to allow freedom of motion.

Plate 60—Assembled Jumping Jack.

Plate 45—Sketch of Assembled Jointed Toys.

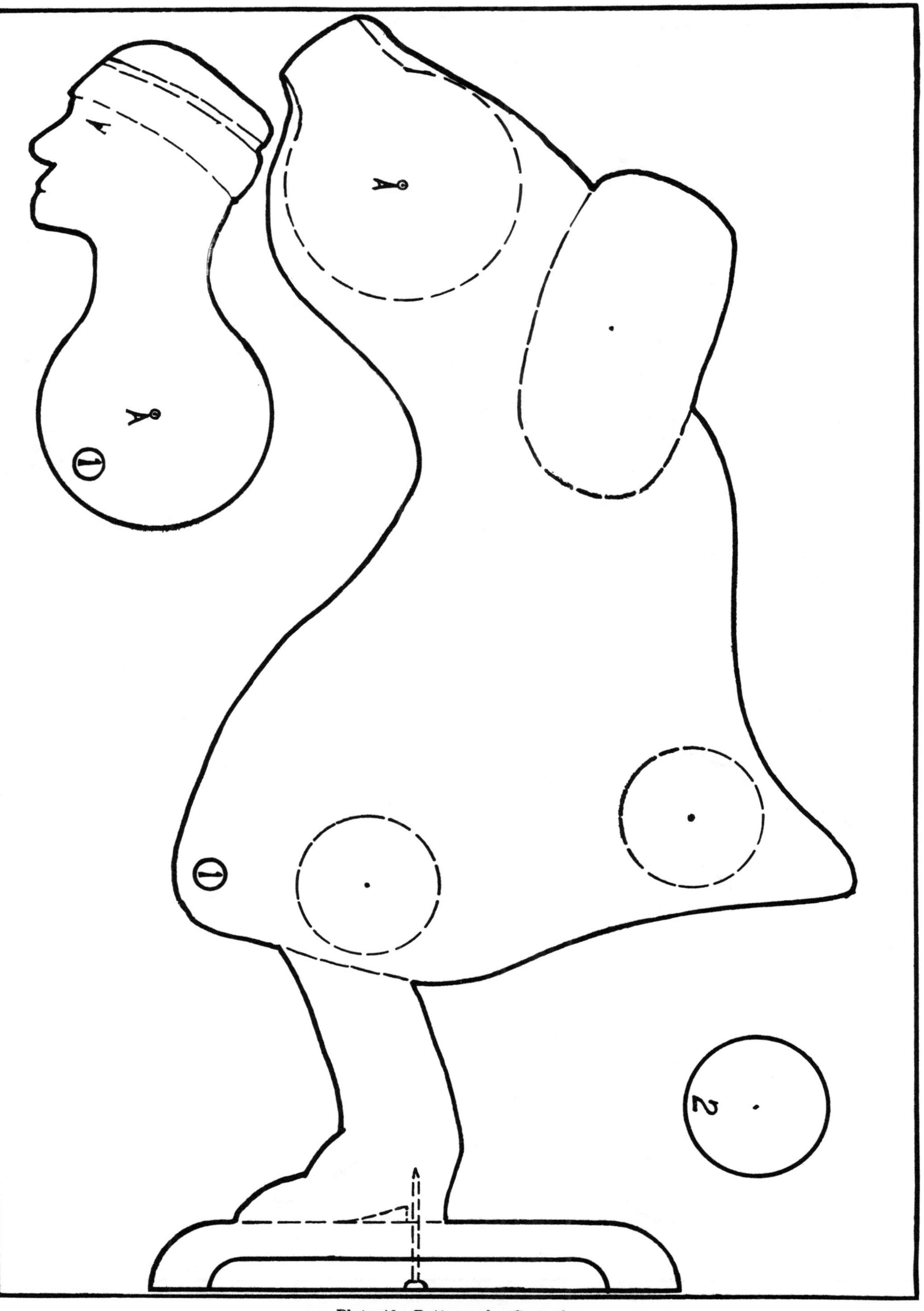

Plate 46—Patterns for Cossack.

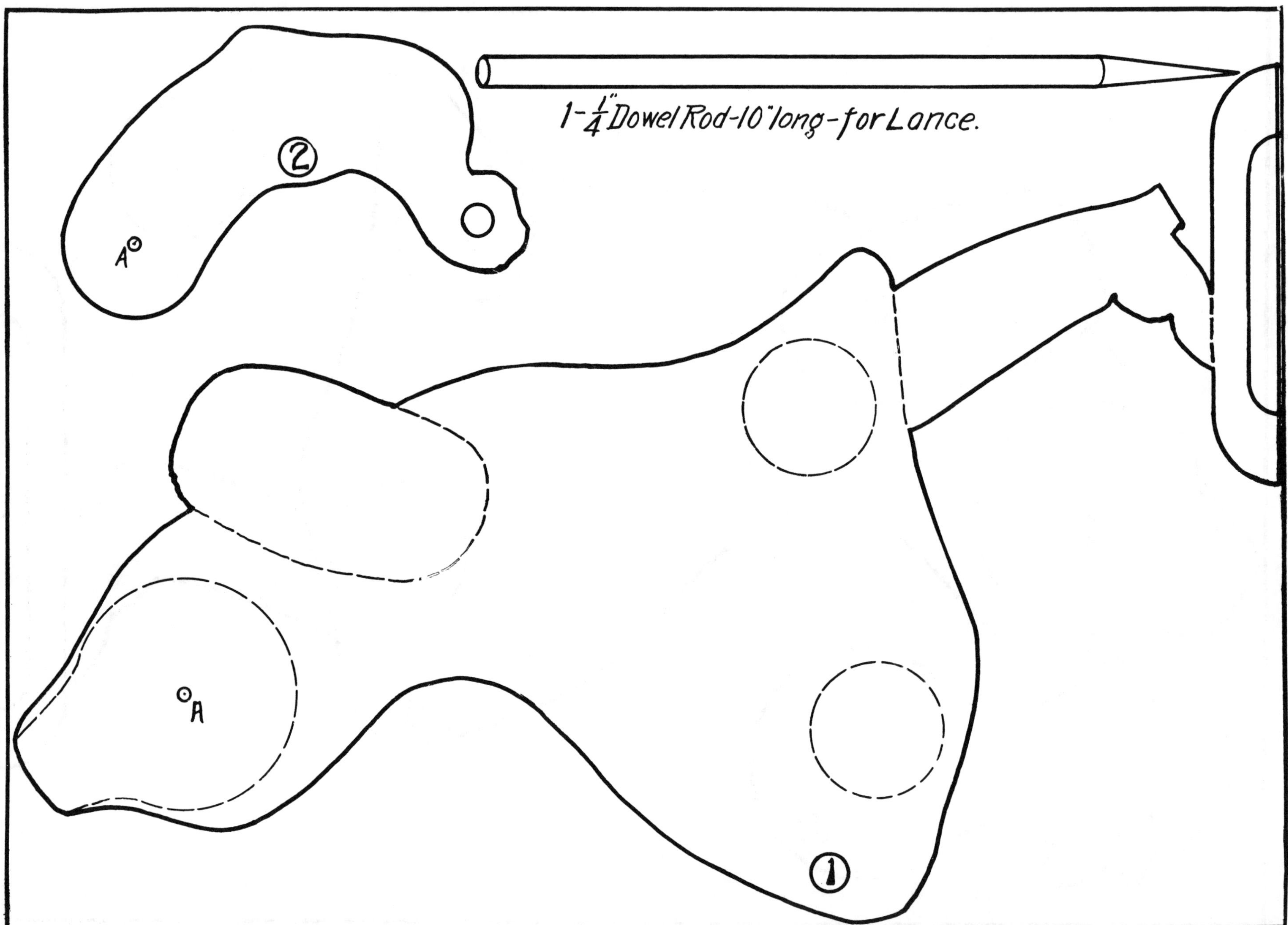

Plate 47—Patterns for Cossack.

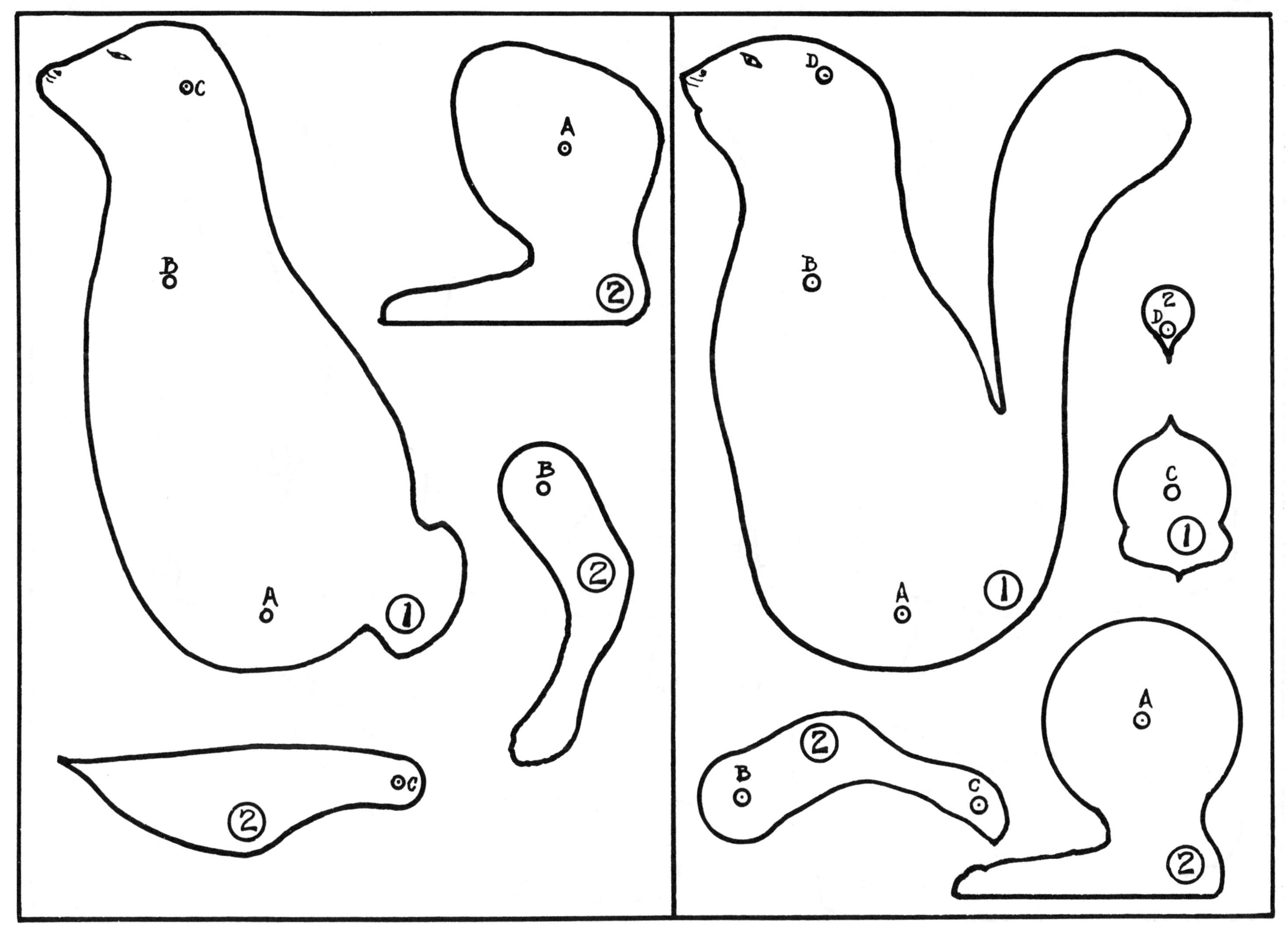

Plate 48—Patterns for Rabbit and Squirrel.

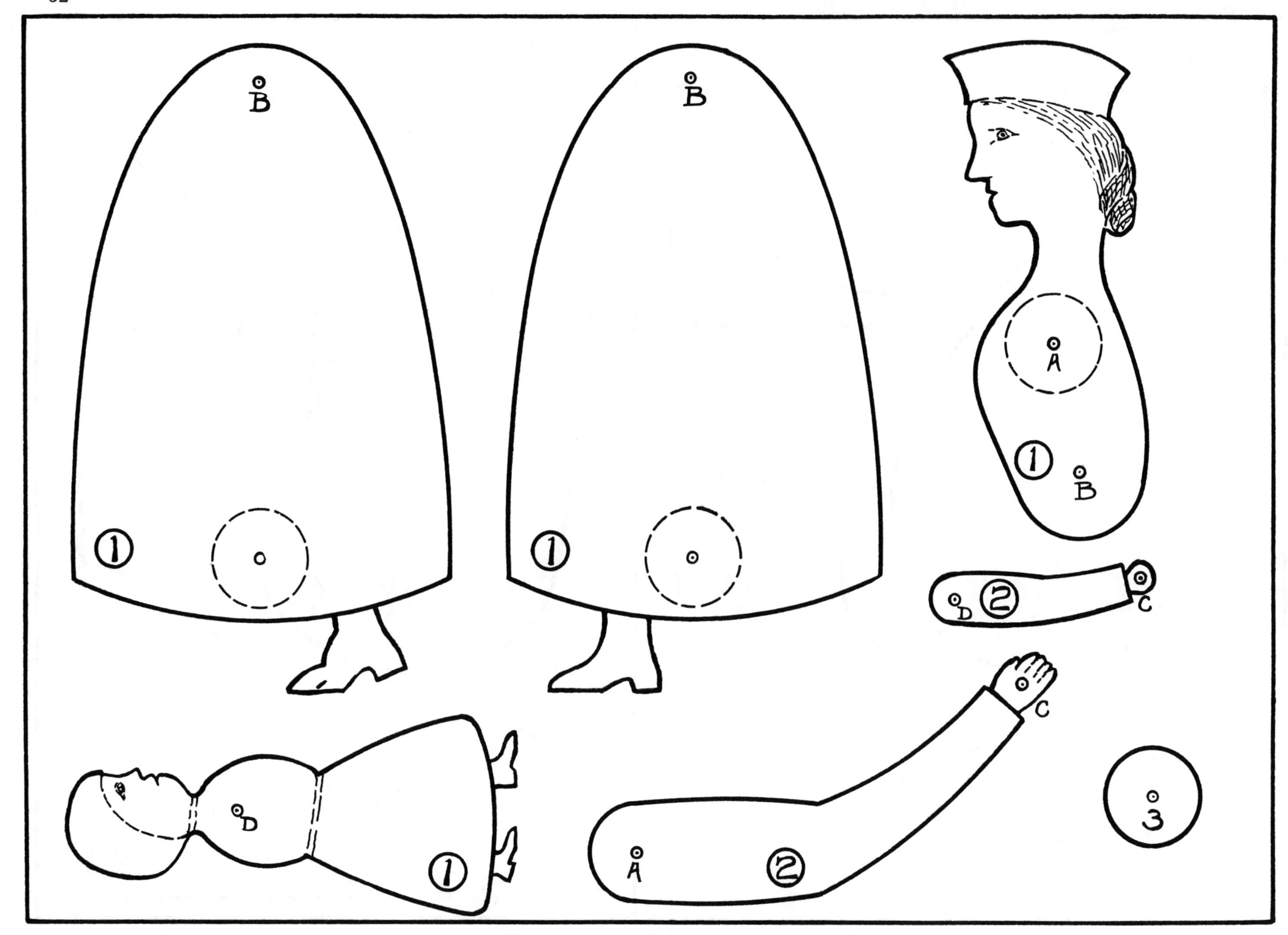

Plate 49—Patterns for Nurse and Child.

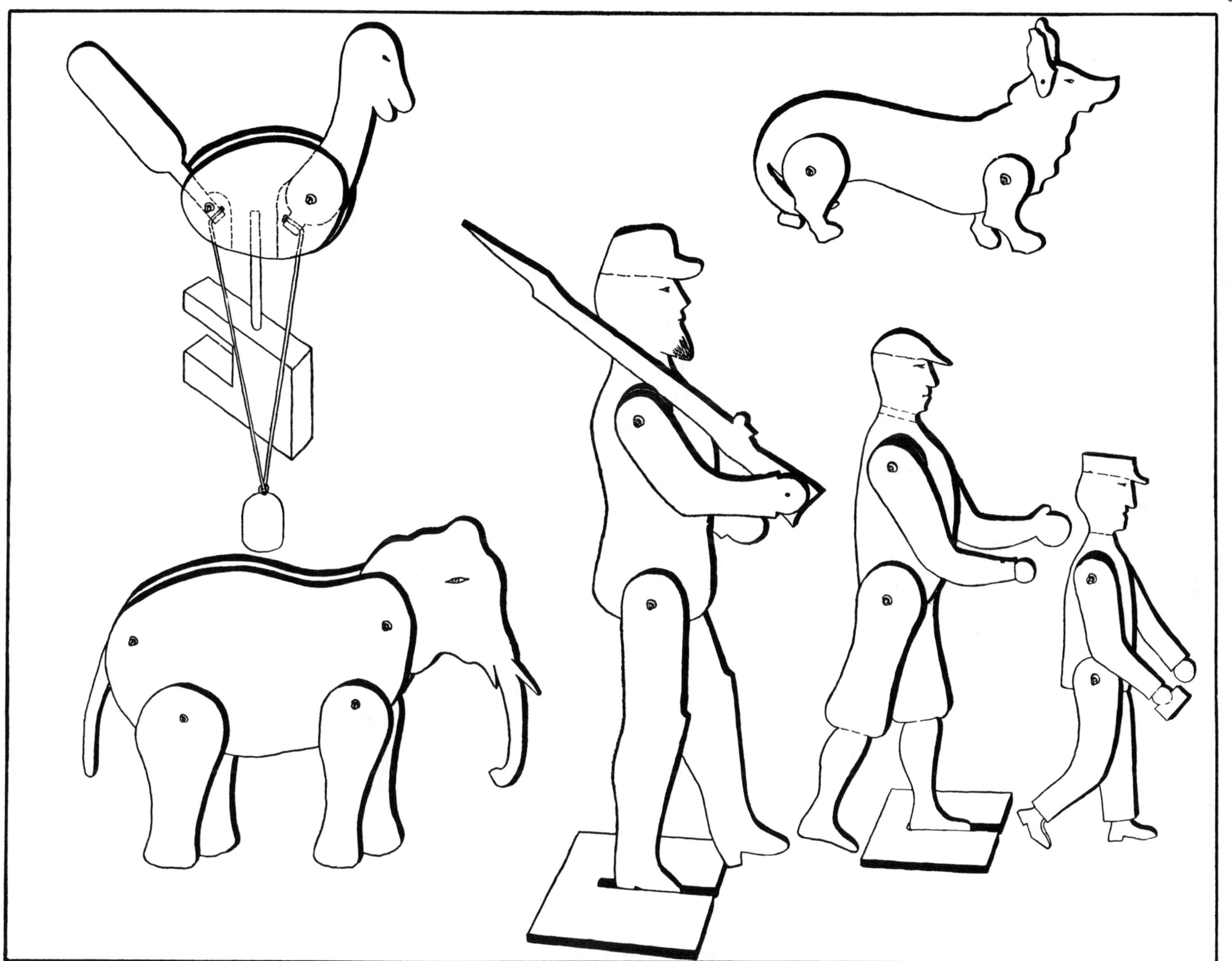

Plate 50—Sketch of Assembled Jointed Toys.

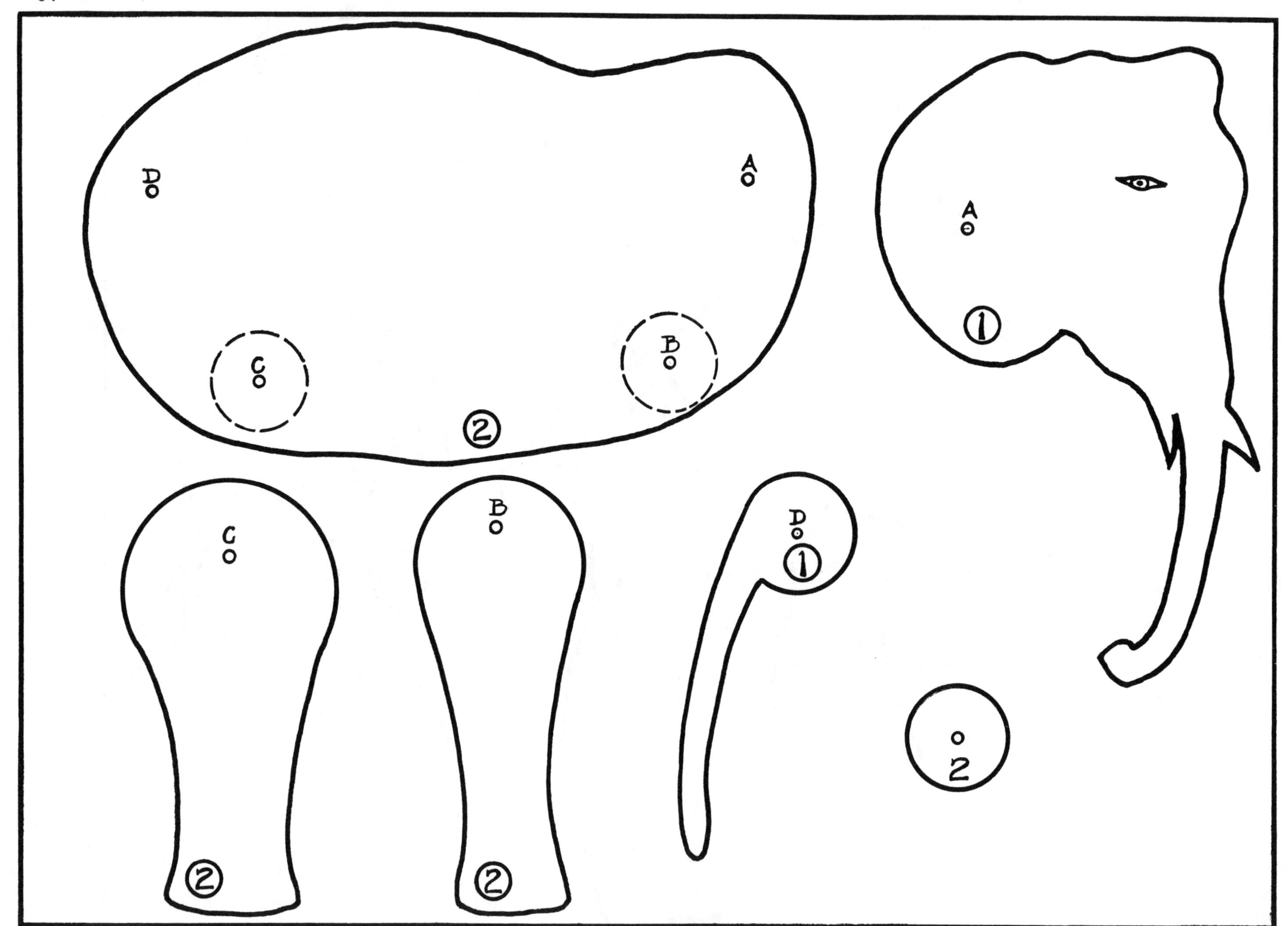

Plate 51—Patterns for Elephant.

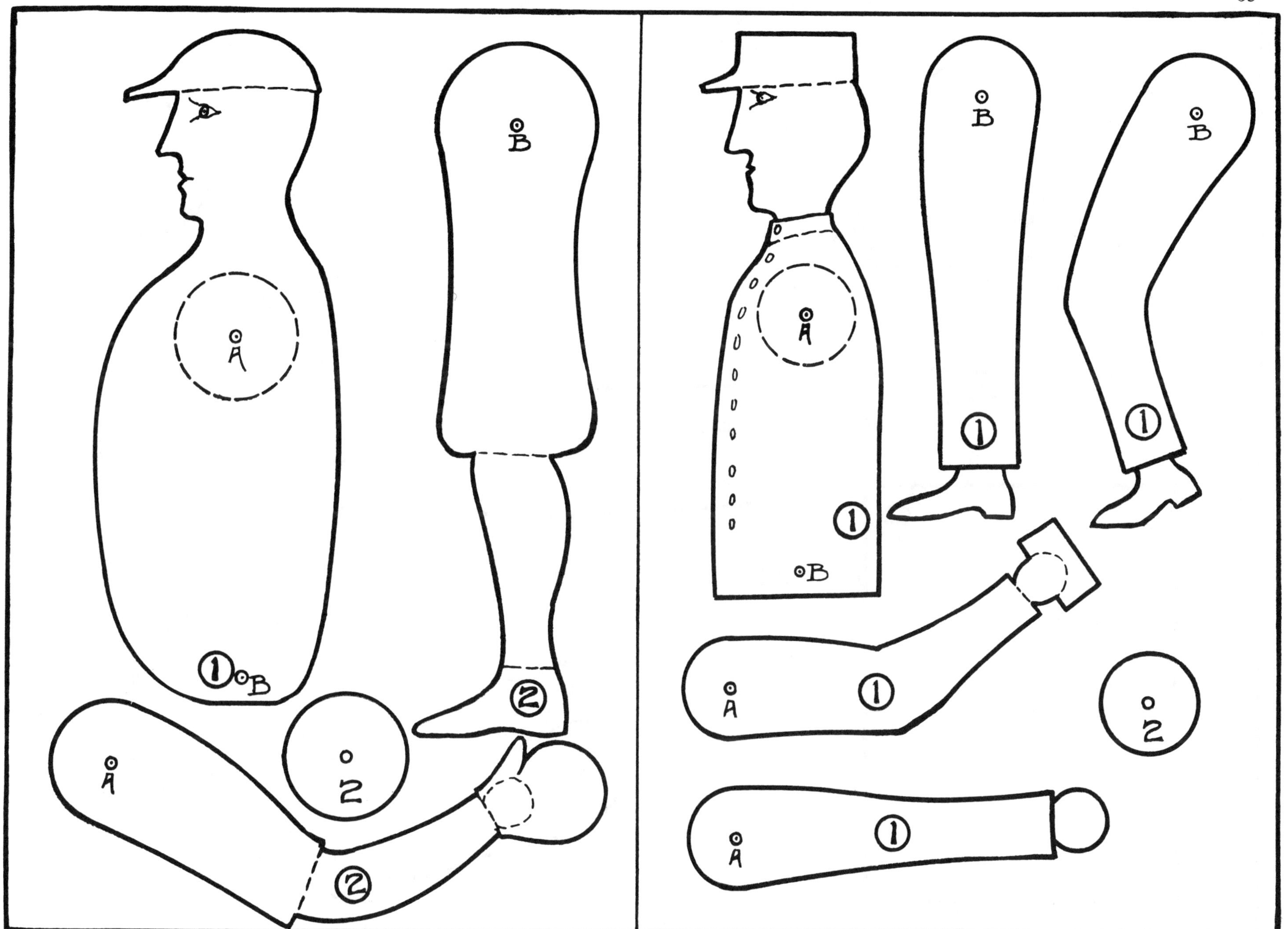

Plate 52—Patterns for Ball Player and Messenger Boy.

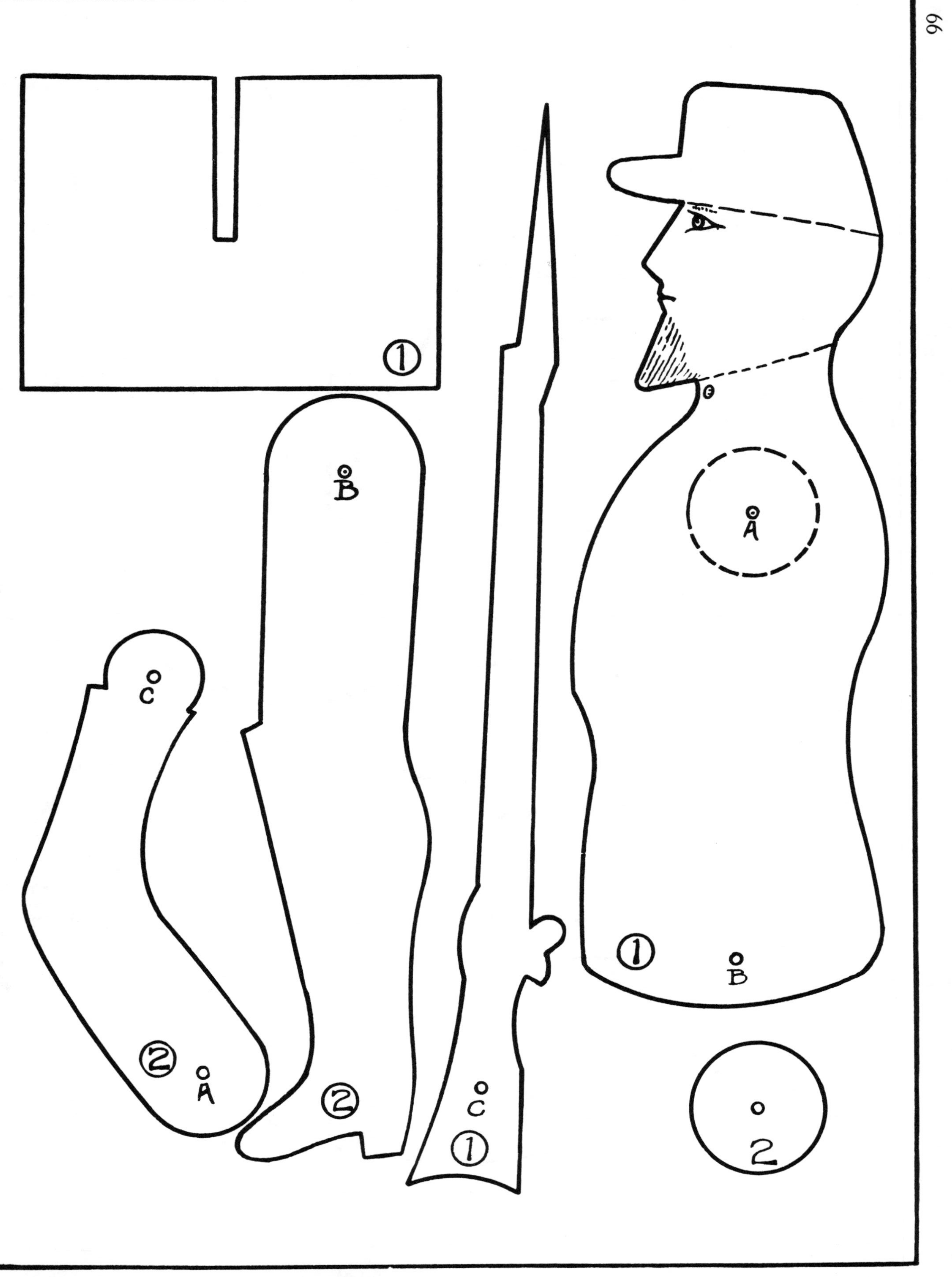

Plate 53—Patterns for French Soldier.

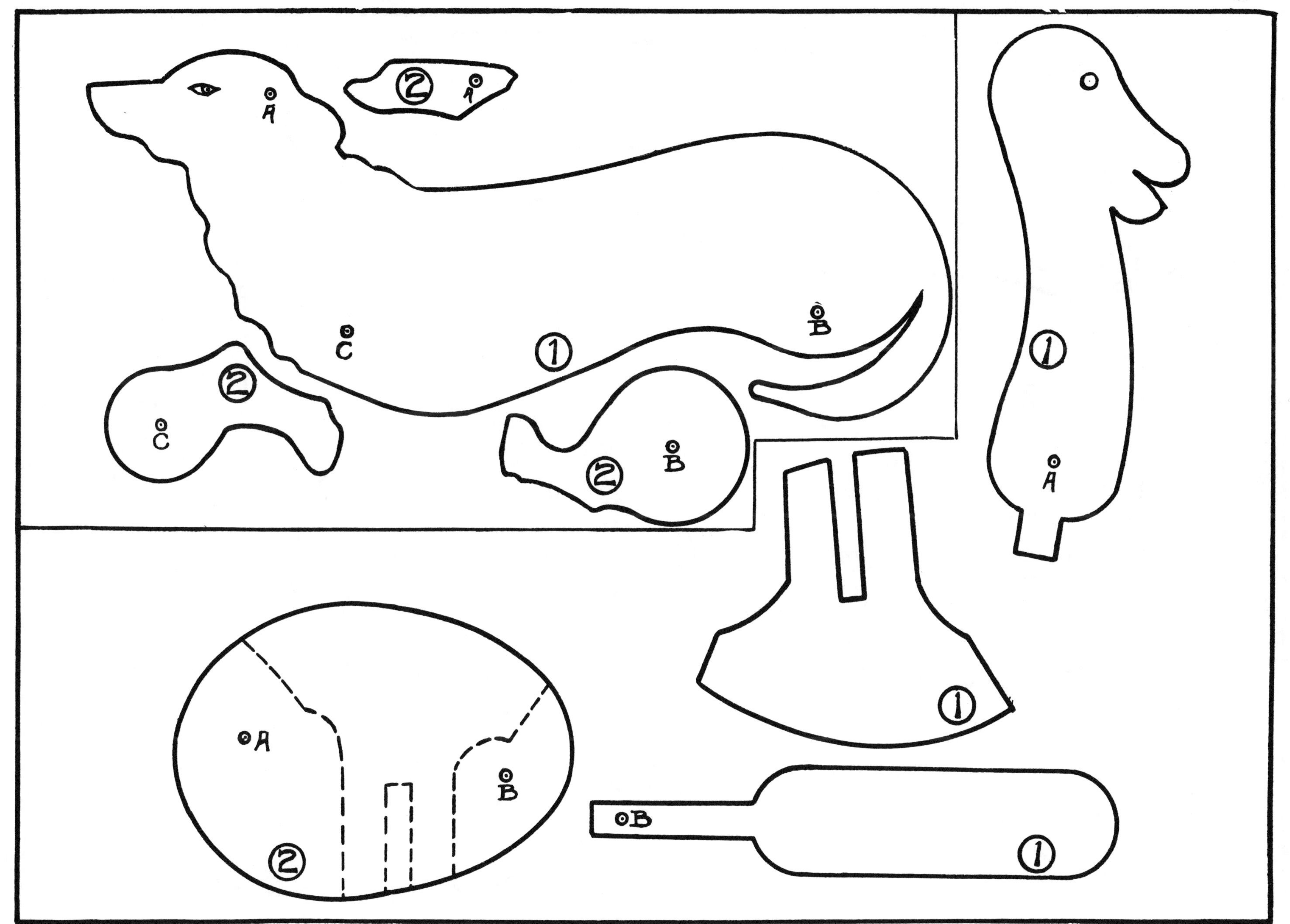

Plate 54—Patterns for Dog and Dodo Bird.

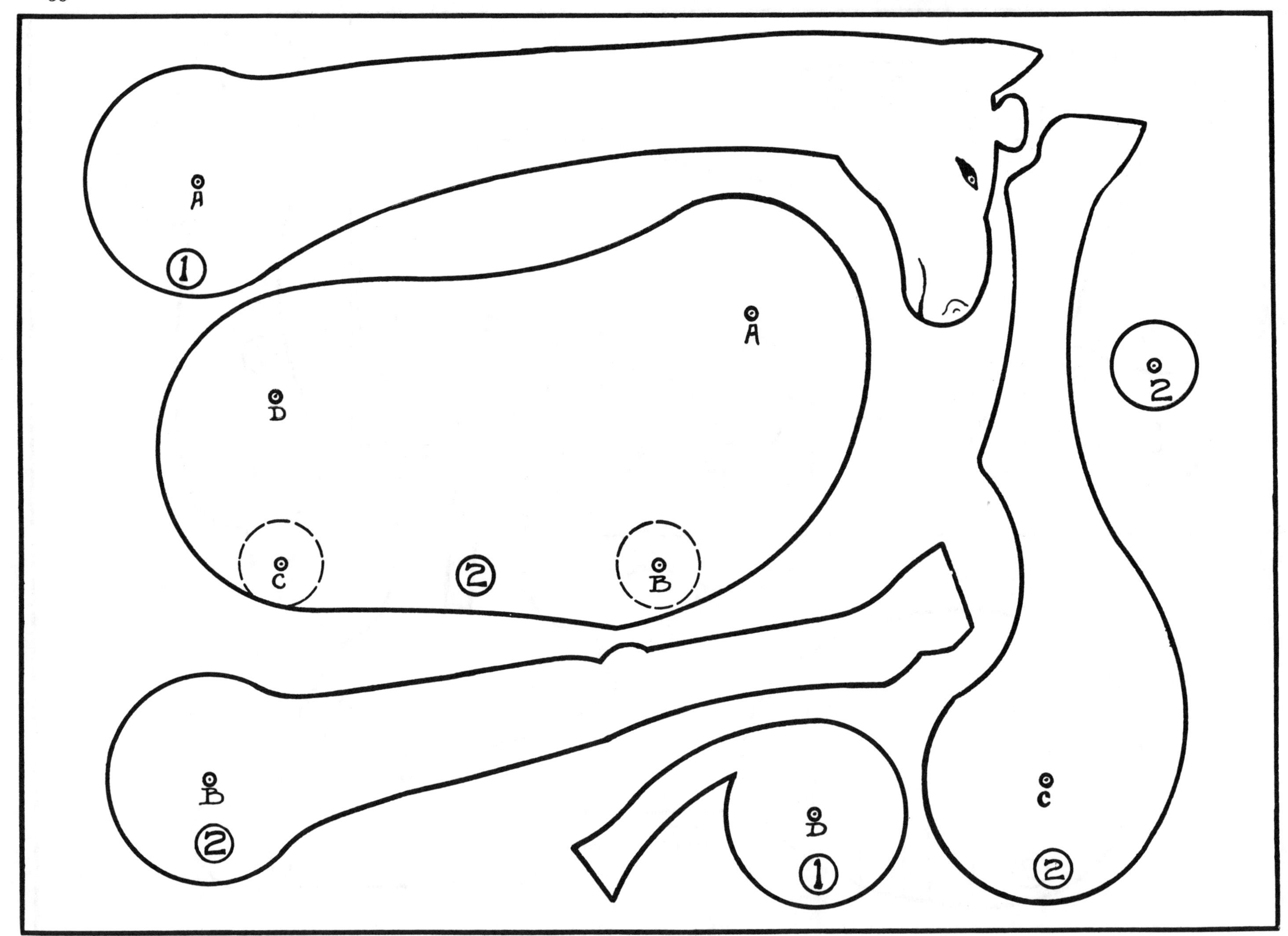

Plate 55—Patterns for Giraffe.

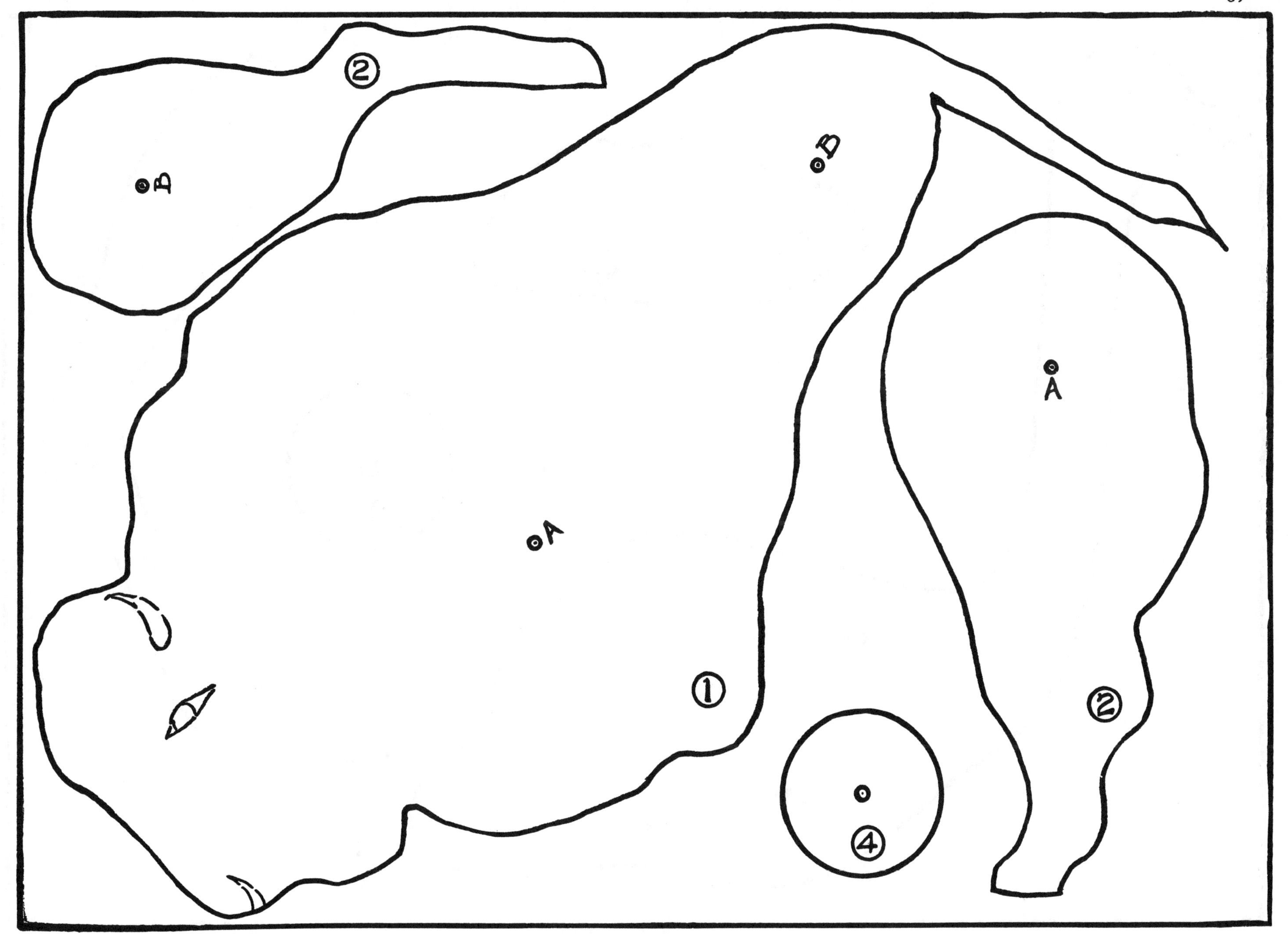

Plate 56—Patterns for Buffalo.

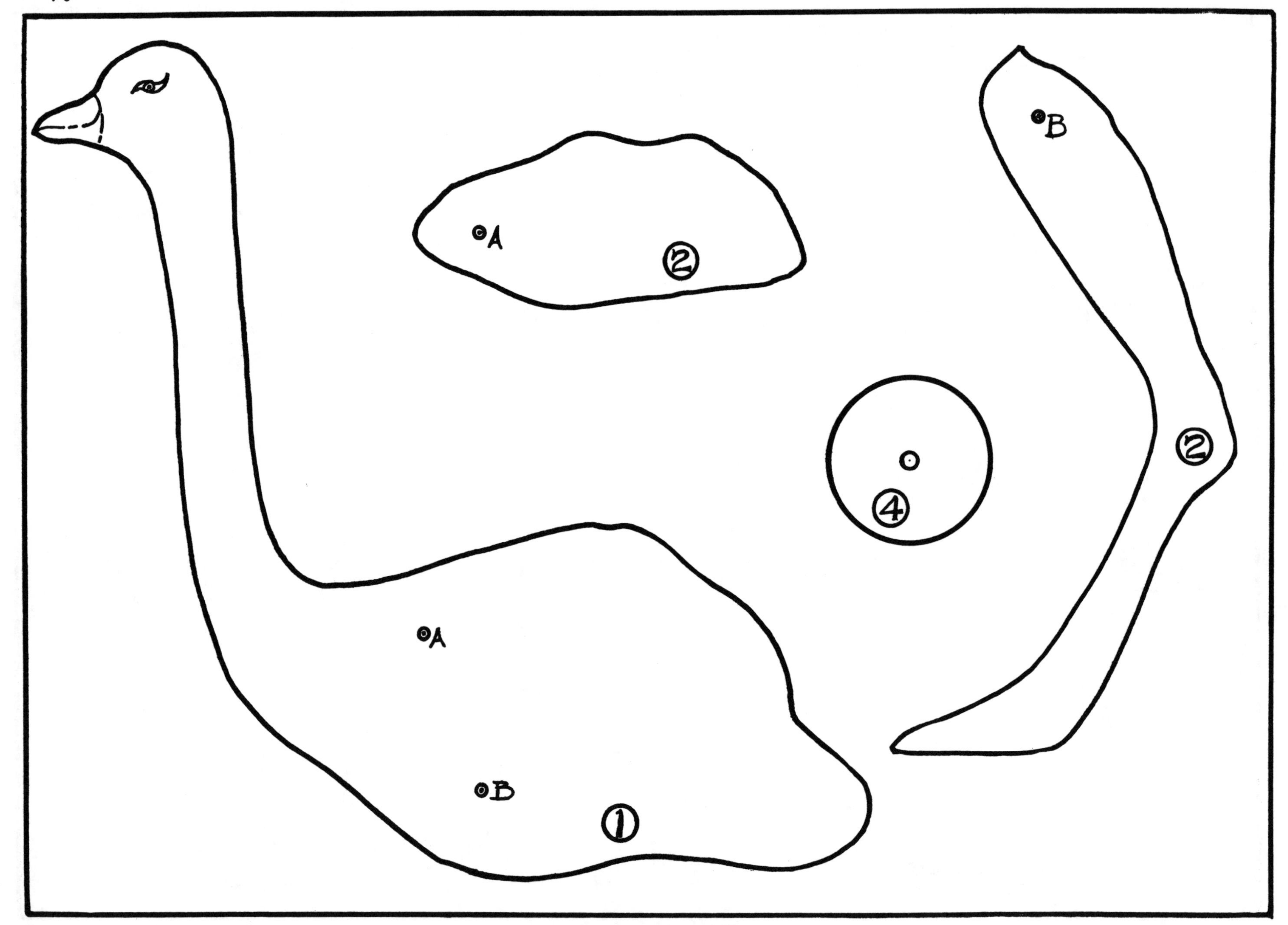

Plate 57—Patterns for Ostrich.

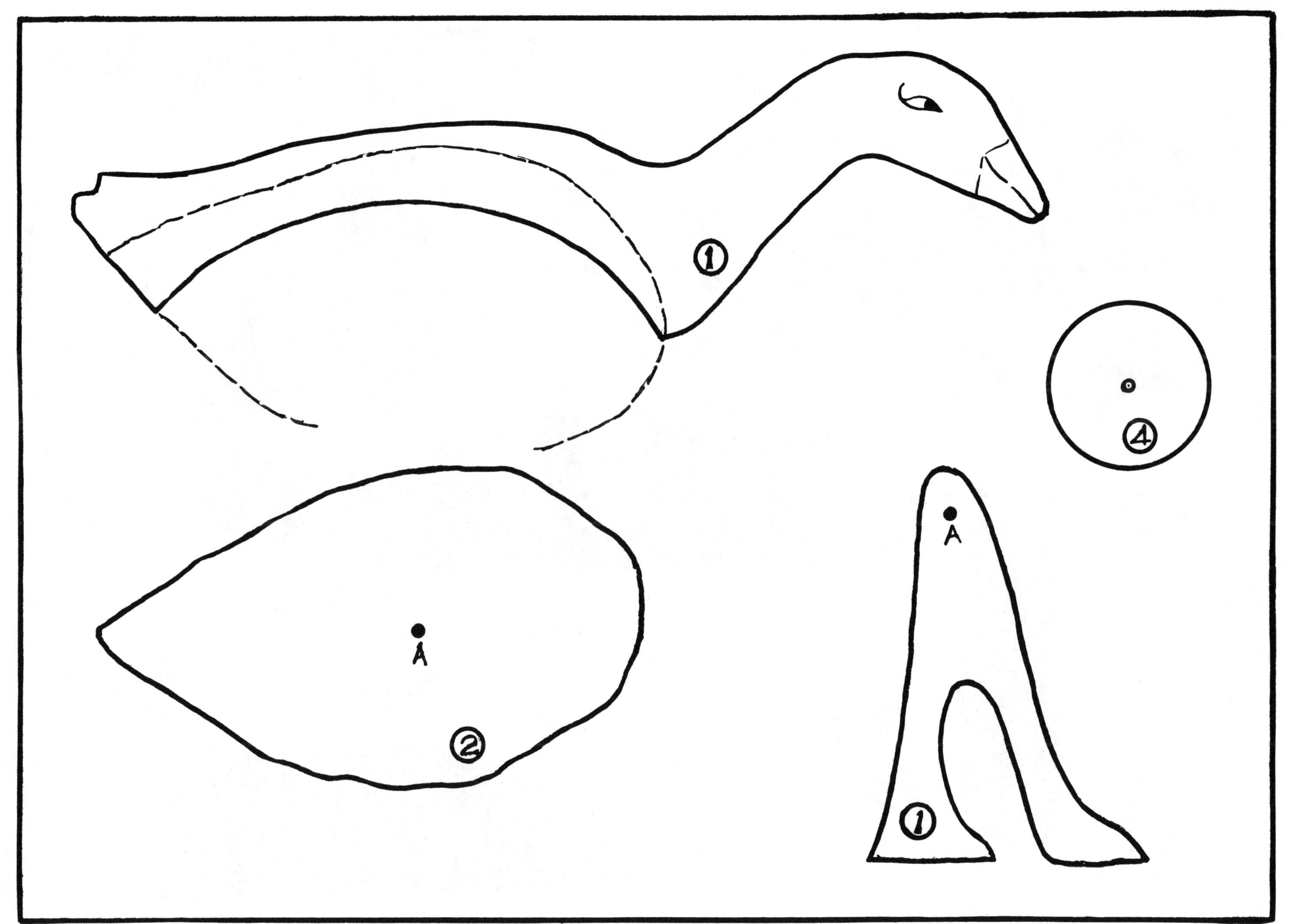

Plate 58—Patterns for Goose.

Plate 59—Detail Parts for Jumping Jack.

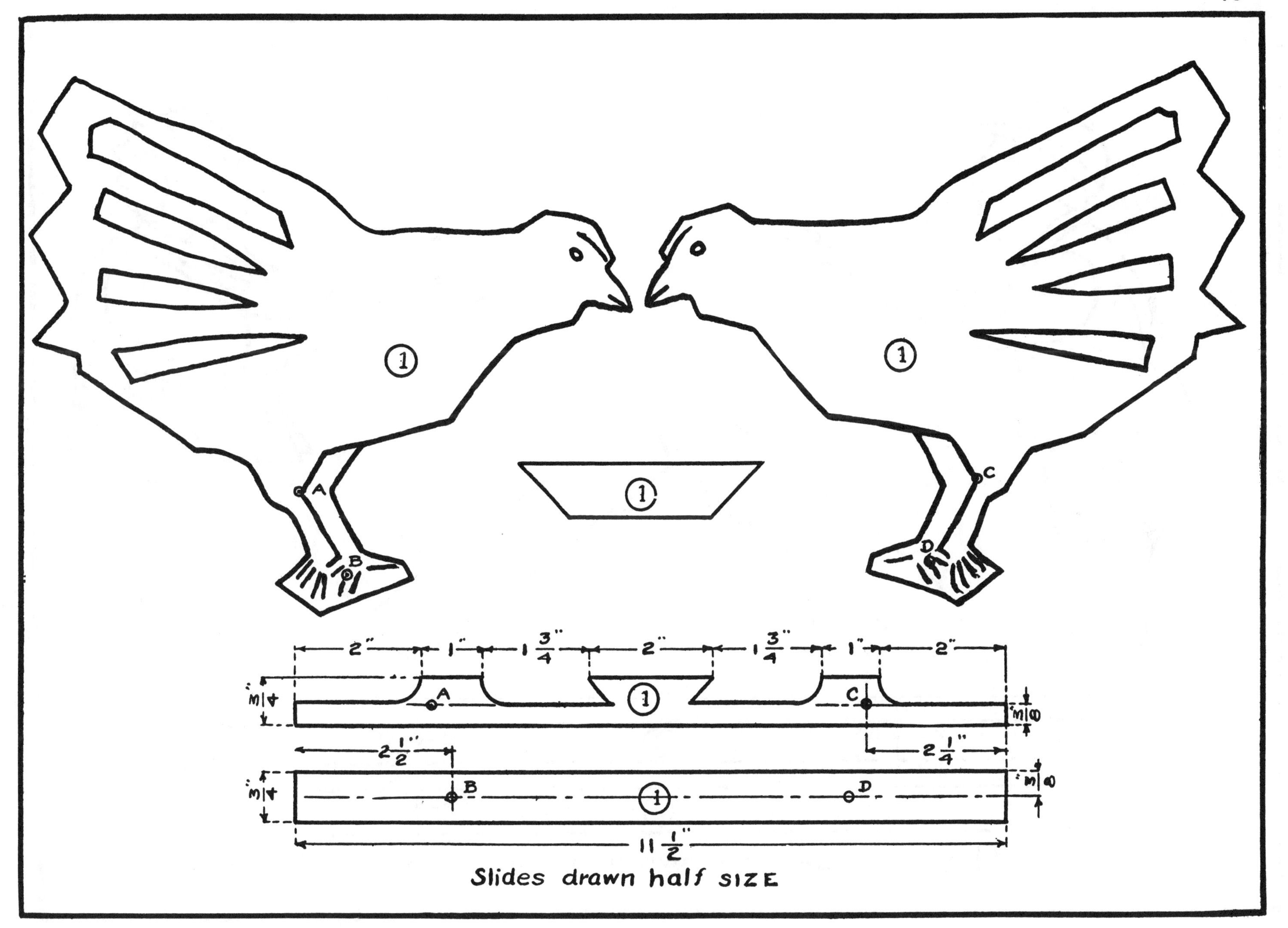

Plate 61—Detail Parts for Feeding Hens.

Plate 62—Detail parts for Wood Choppers.

By holding the lower strip and pulling and pushing the upper strip, the hens will alternately peck at the disk. The toy when brightly colored is most interesting.

THE WOOD CHOPPERS

Plate 62 is the working drawing for two Wood Choppers. The Choppers themselves are shown full size, while the slide on which they are worked is only one-half size. Plate 63 shows the various parts assembled. The Wood Choppers are worked in the same ways as the Feeding Hens.

PARALLEL-MOVEMENT TOYS

The eight movable toys illustrated and described next are constructed on the same principles as the Feeding Hens and the Wood Choppers. It will be observed that a full-size drawing is given for each of the parts of each toy, while the assembled toy is drawn on a small scale.

FEEDING BIRDS

The most complicated mechanical toy in the collection is that of the Feeding Birds. Plate 73 is a detailed drawing of the connections necessary to produce the desired result. Plate 74 shows the parts assembled. The birds are colored to represent red-headed woodpeckers. The full-size drawing of the bird is shown in Plate 76.

FIGHTING CAT AND DOG

The Fighting Cat and Dog toy, shown in Plate 77, is somewhat simpler in construction than the Feeding Birds.

DOLL-HOUSE FURNITURE

Plate 80 shows a number of interesting and novel pieces of doll furniture which may be constructed to furnish a doll house. The construction is very simple, being of the butt-joint type, fastened with small brads and glue. The furniture should be stained rather than painted, with the exception of the Cat Chair and Duck Rocker, which should be painted as the animals previously described were painted.

Plate 74—Feeding Birds.

After the children have constructed the furniture from the patterns given, they should be led to construct similar pieces from their own designs.

Plates 63-64—Assembled Wood Choppers and Feeding Hens.

Plate 65—Pattern for Fish and Ducks.

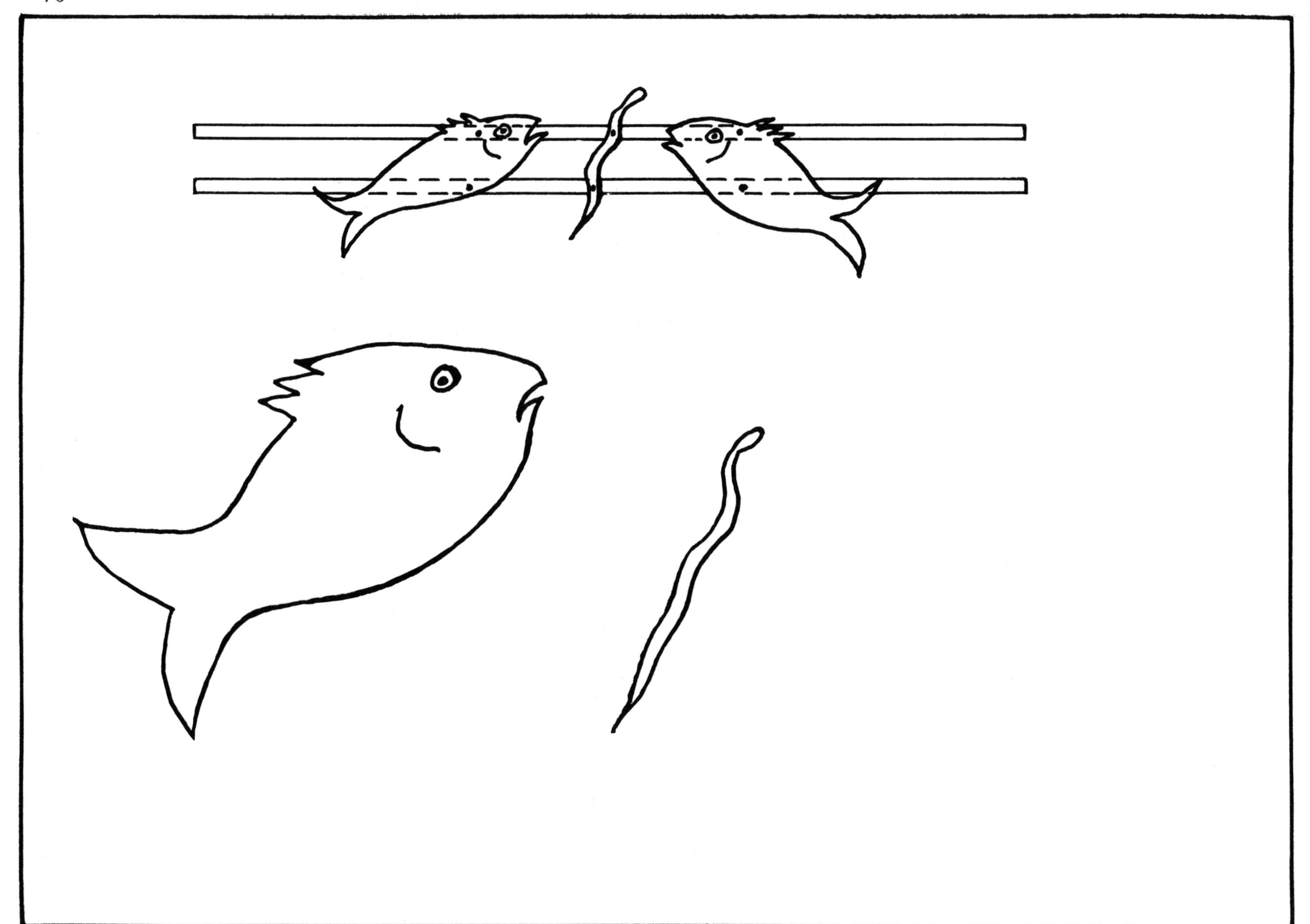

Plate 66—Pattern for Hungry Fish.

Plate 67—Pattern for Mice and Cheese.

Plate 68—Pattern for Boxing Foxes.

Plate 69—Pattern for Boxers.

Plate 70—Pattern for the Bears and Apple.

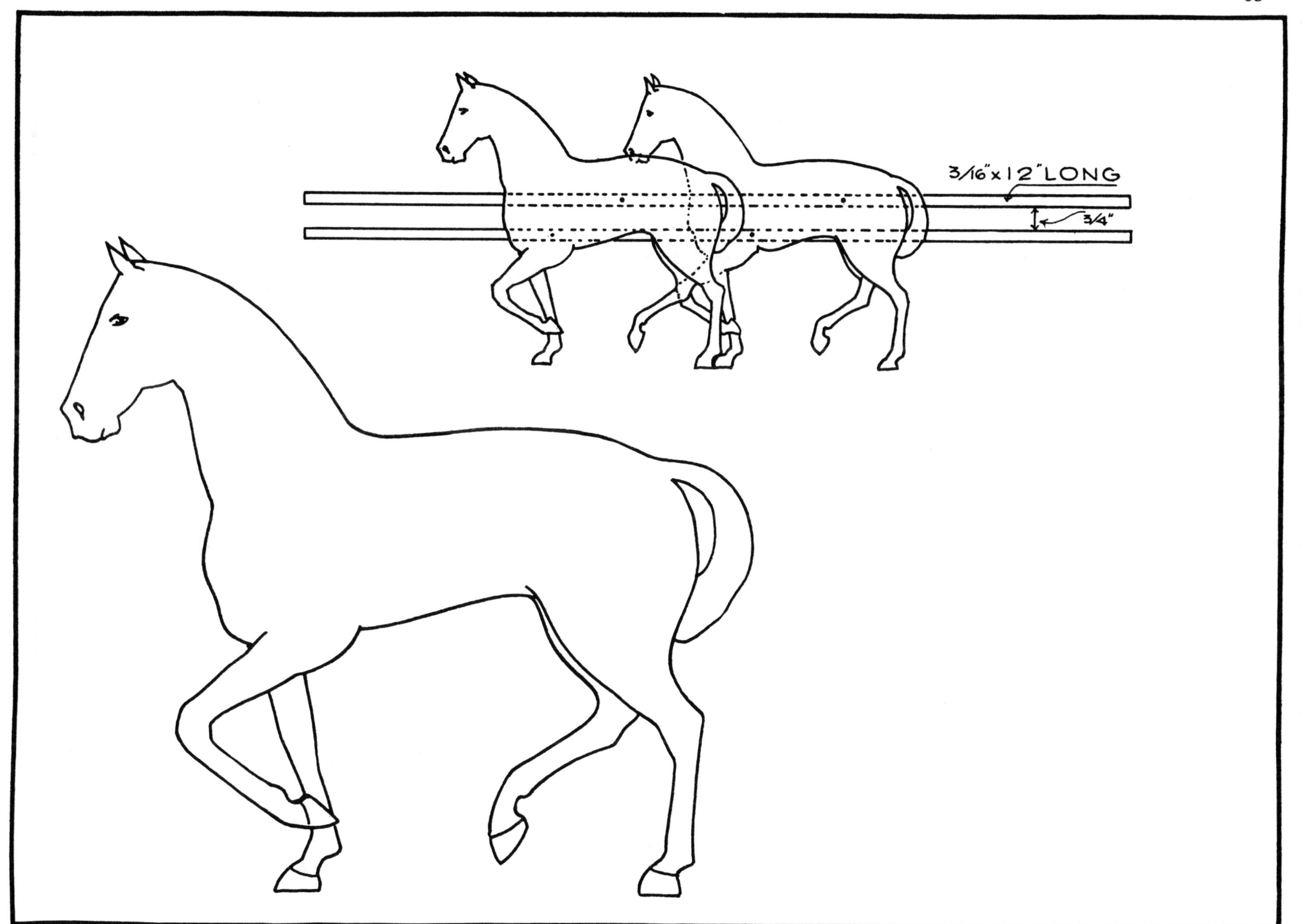

Plate 71—Pattern for Racing Horses.

Plate 72—Pattern for Antelope and Indian.

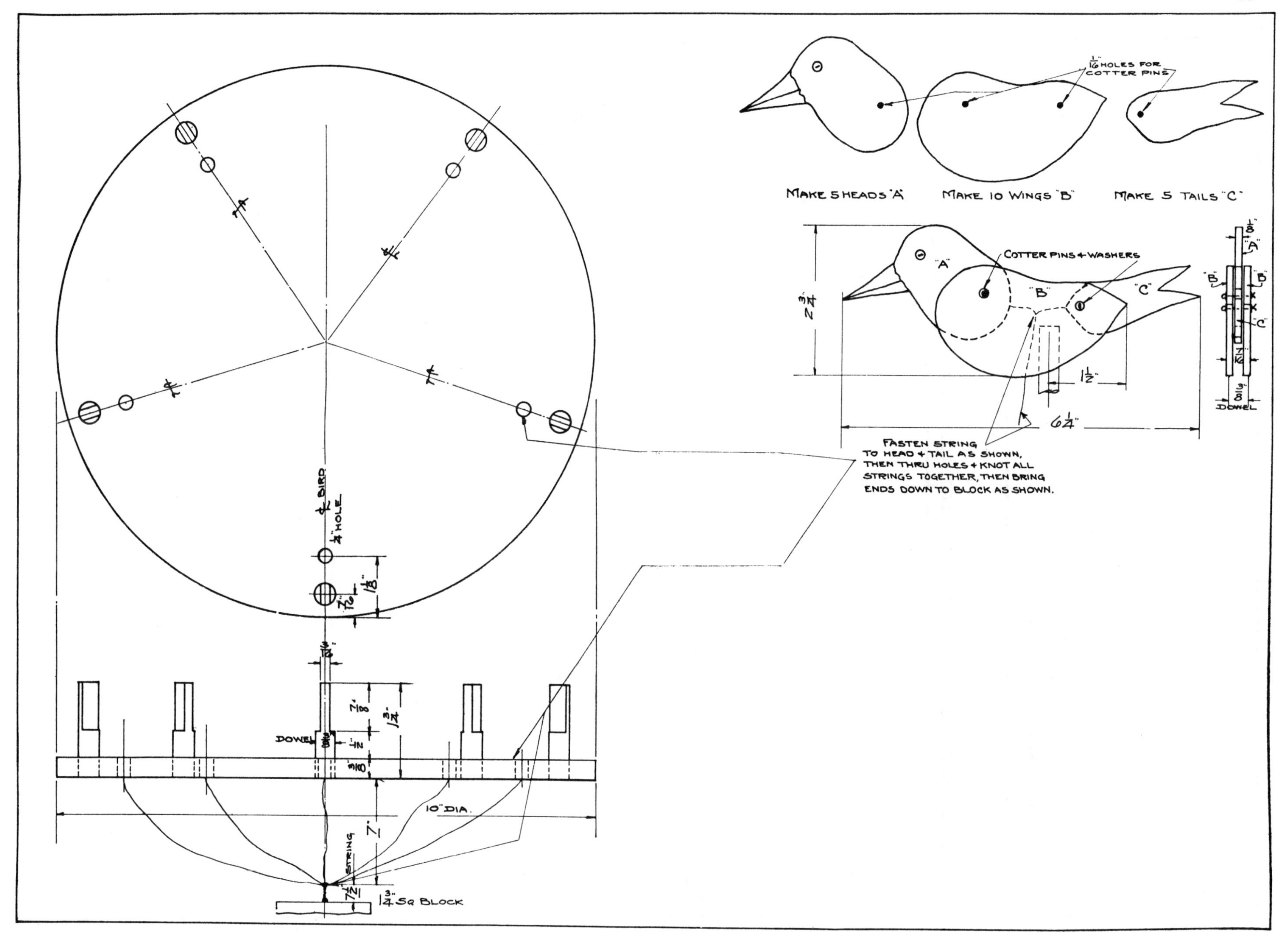

Plate 73—Details of Feeding Birds.

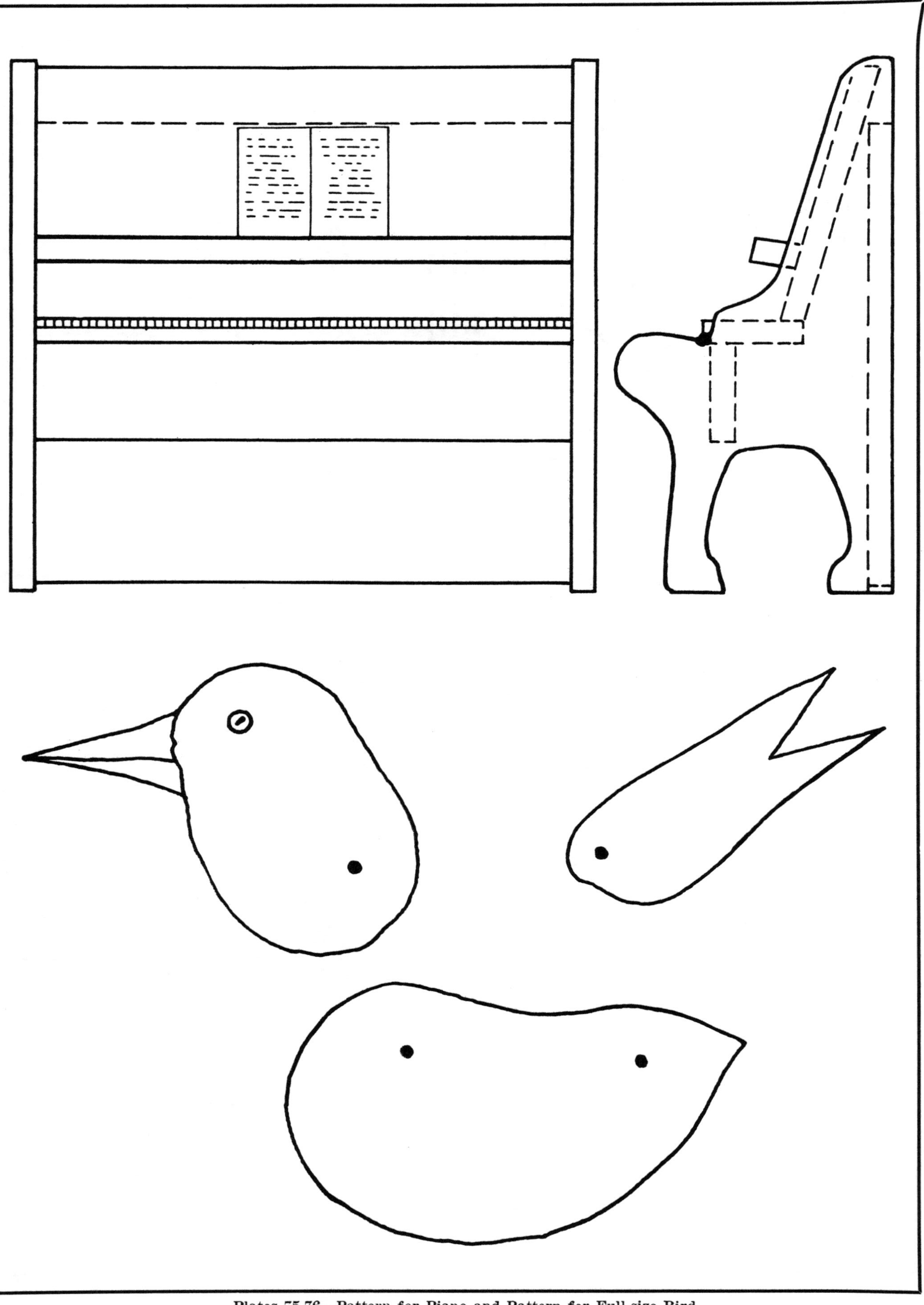

Plates 75-76—Pattern for Piano and Pattern for Full-size Bird.

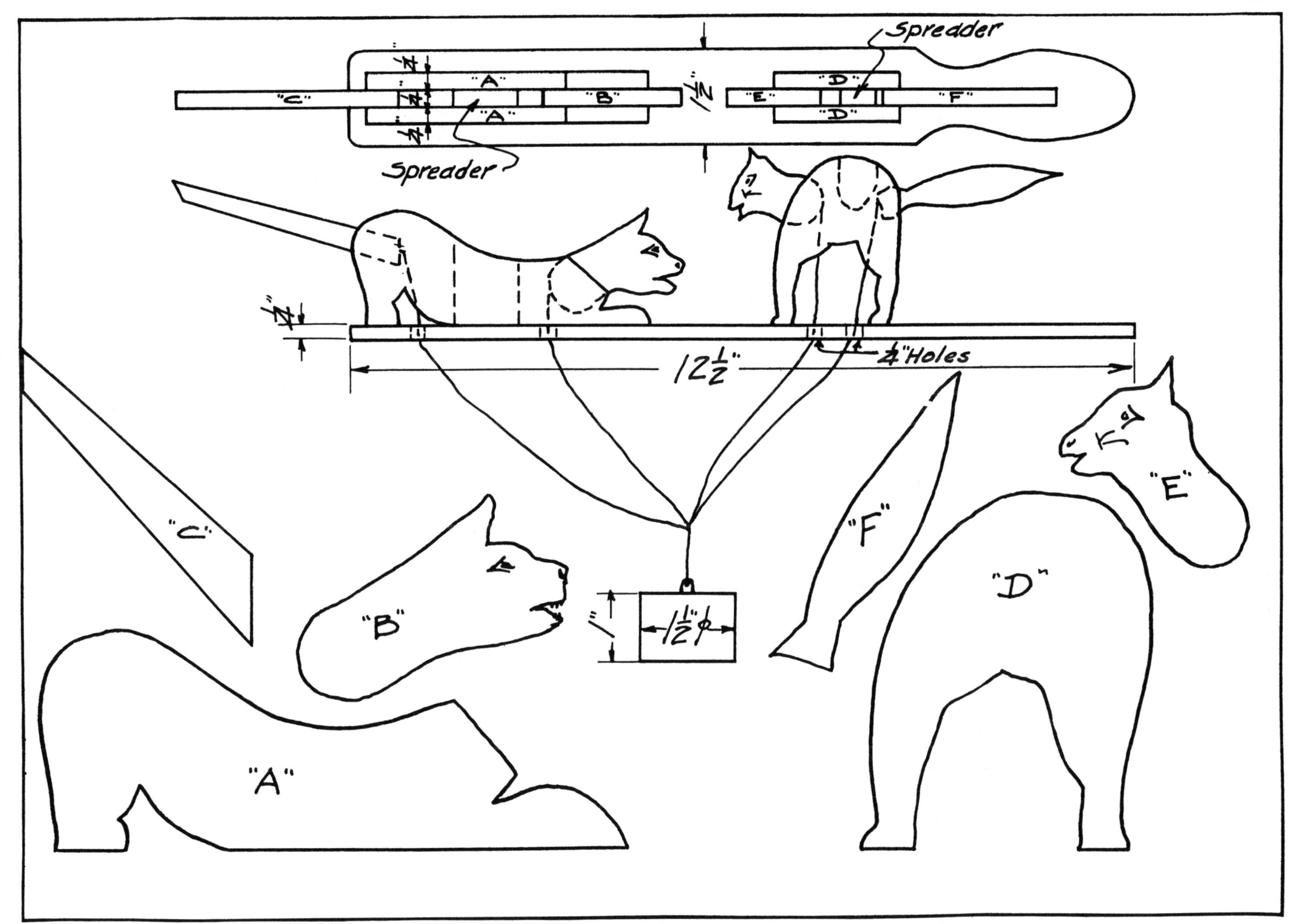

Plate 77—Pattern for Fighting Cat and Dog.

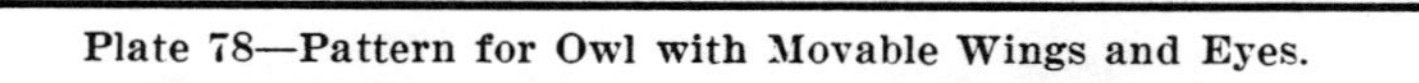

Plate 78—Pattern for Owl with Movable Wings and Eyes.

Plate 79—Pattern for Duck with Movable Bill and Wing.

Plate 81 gives the patterns for the Chair shown in the upper left-hand corner of Plate 80. Again, the numbers on the patterns represent the number of pieces to be made from each pattern. The dotted lines show where the different pieces are to be placed when assembling the furniture. It is essential to have the edges of the pieces square, or as nearly square as is possible with the tools at hand, because the success of the butt joint as a joint depends upon how square the edges are cut. When sandpapering an edge or end of a piece of wood that is to be square, place a large sheet of sandpaper face up, on a perfectly flat surface. Then run the edge or end to be sanded, over the sandpaper, first being sure that the piece is held at right angles with the sandpaper.

Plate 82 gives the patterns for the Table illustrated in the upper left-hand corner of Plate 80. It is very simple in construction and is of the same type of furniture as the Chair.

Plate 83 contains the patterns for the Cradle shown in the upper right-hand corner of Plate 80. First make two pieces from the pattern for the sides; then make two pieces from the pattern for the back, leaving one 1/4 inch longer than the other. Now take the longer back and cut off a piece 2 11/16 inches from the upper edge, as shown in the pattern. This will make the top of the cradle; the remaining piece will make the front. The bottom, not shown in the drawing, consists of a straight rectangular piece 3 5/8 inches wide by 6 inches long. By this time the pupils should be able to cut out pieces like this without a pattern.

This might be a good place to introduce the use of the try-square in marking off parallel lines, and in checking up edges and ends that are to be squared. The teacher should explain to the class the function and proper use of the try-square, so that each child will understand it thoroughly before using it.

The patterns for the Cat Chair and Duck Rocker are given in Plates 84 and 85. These are interesting pieces of furniture and fit very well in the nursery of a doll house.

Plate 86 illustrates the patterns for the Rocker shown in the lower right-hand corner of Plate 80. A straight chair can be made from the same patterns by omitting the rocker, and cutting the bottom of the legs square.

Plate 87 gives the patterns for the Table and Chairs shown in the lower right-hand corner of Plate 80. This, with a few duplicates of the chairs, makes a very neat set.

TOY VEHICLES

Toy vehicles afford another opportunity for making objects of light wood. Plate 91 shows a number of toy vehicles constructed of light wood. The construction of these toys is very elementary. It is the same as that used in the doll furniture; that is, butt-joint construction, fastened with small brads and glue. The only new construction is that of the wheels and axles.

In Plate 92 is shown the method used in fastening the wheels to the axle. The wheel is made first, then two smaller circles, which are used as hubs, are cut. The hub is fastened securely to the wheel by means of small brads and glue, and then the wheel is fastened to the axle by driving a long brad through the hub into the dowel rod which serves as axle.

Plate 92 gives the patterns for an Automobile Delivery Truck. The only patterns shown are the side and wheels. This is all that is necessary, as the other parts are all straight, rectangular pieces. A list of the pieces and their names is given. The dotted lines show where the pieces go in the assembling of the truck.

Plate 93 gives the patterns for the Wheelbarrow shown in the upper right-hand corner of Plate 91. Small pieces are cut out of the wheels, so that it has the appearance of having

Plate 80—Sketches of Toy Furniture.

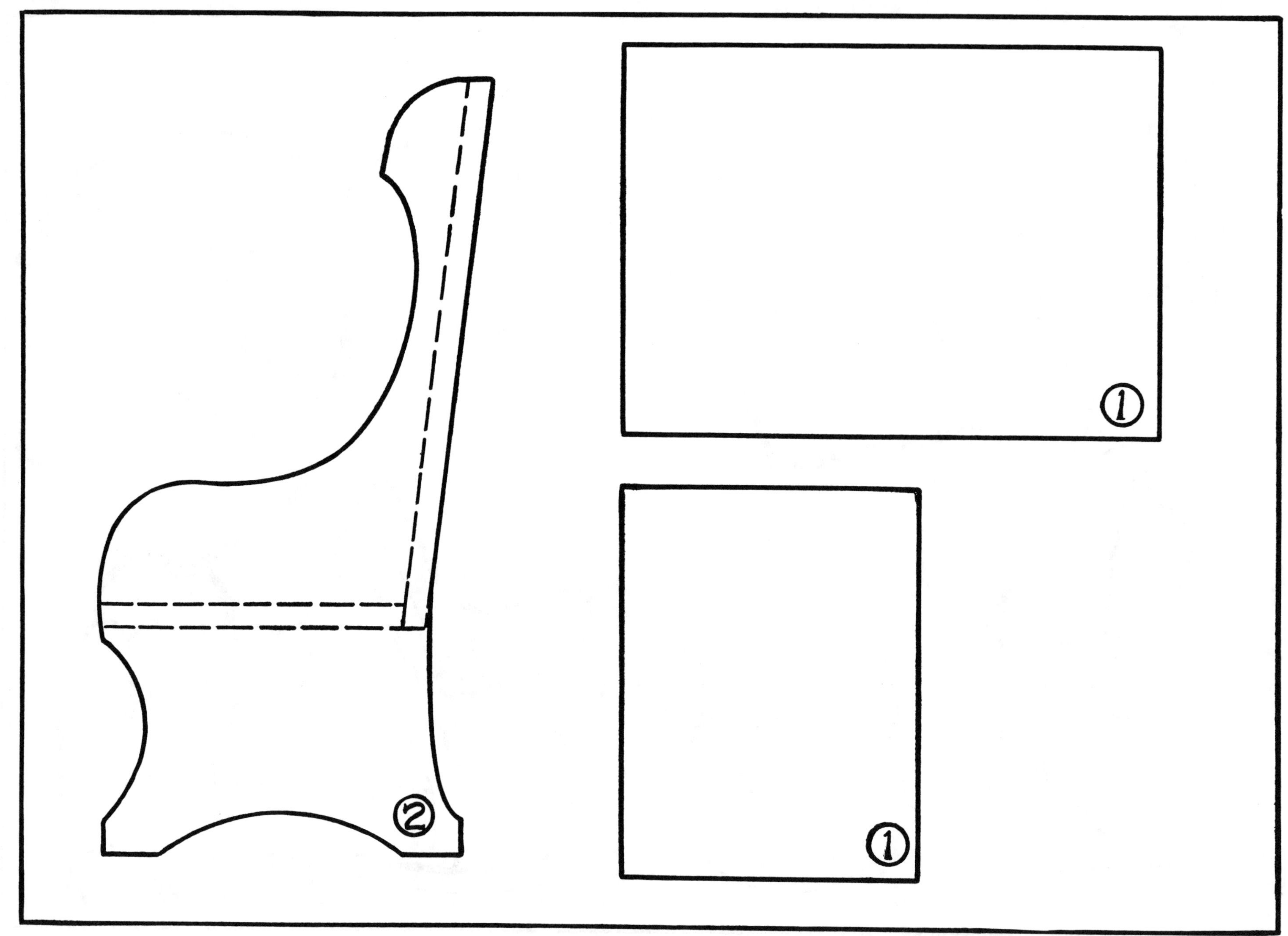

Plate 81—Patterns for Chair.

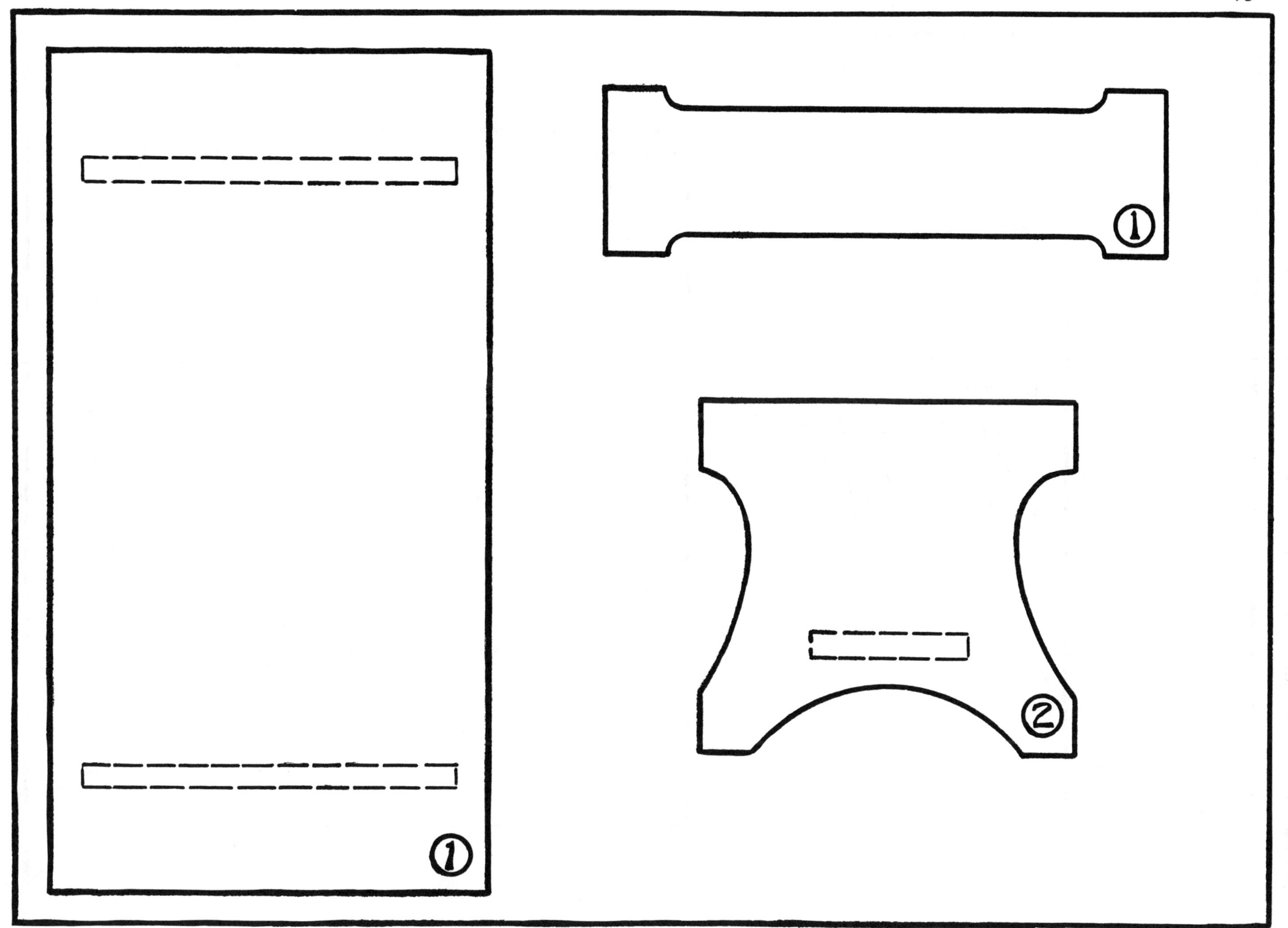

Plate 82—Patterns for Library Table.

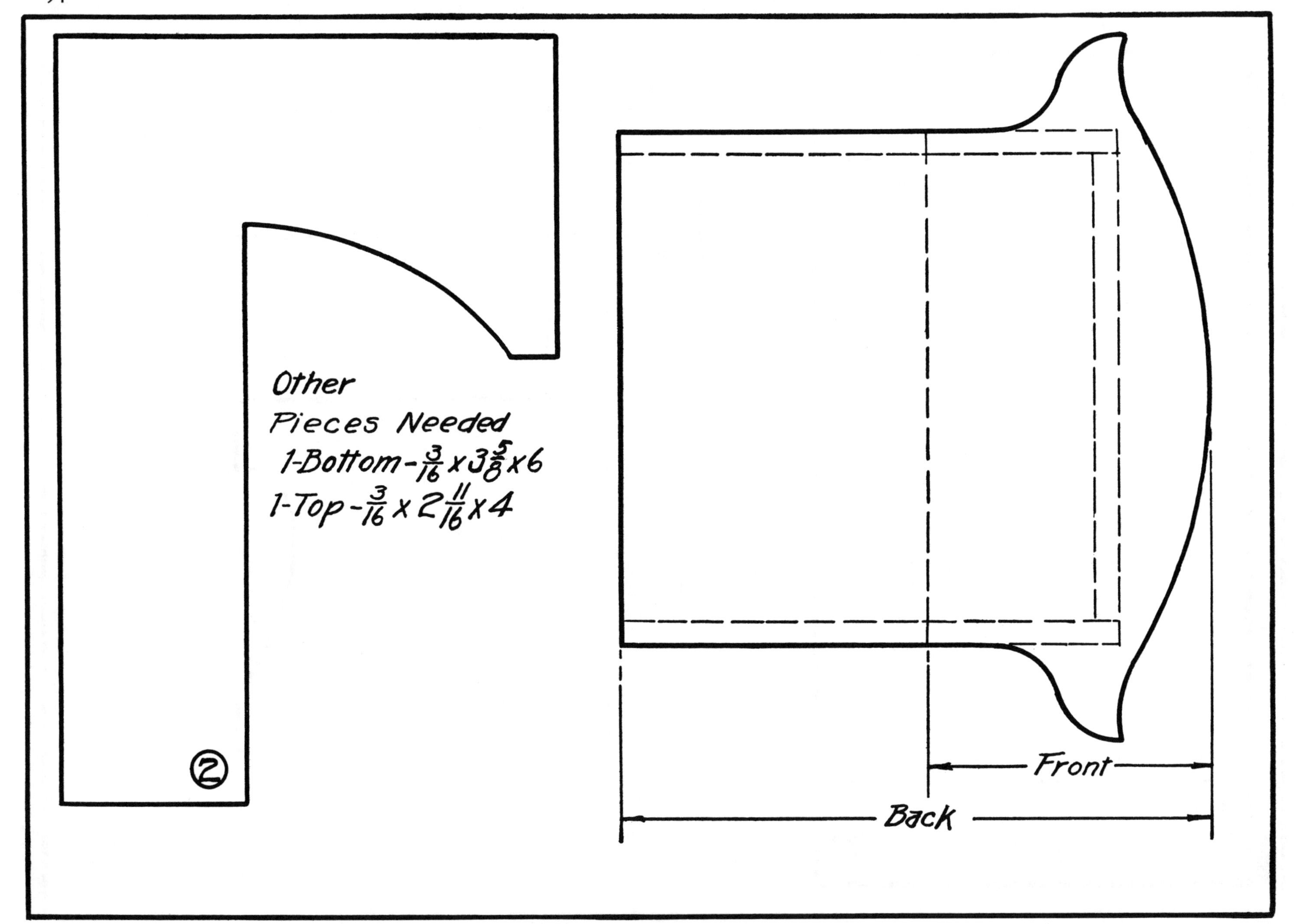

Plate 83—Patterns for Cradle.

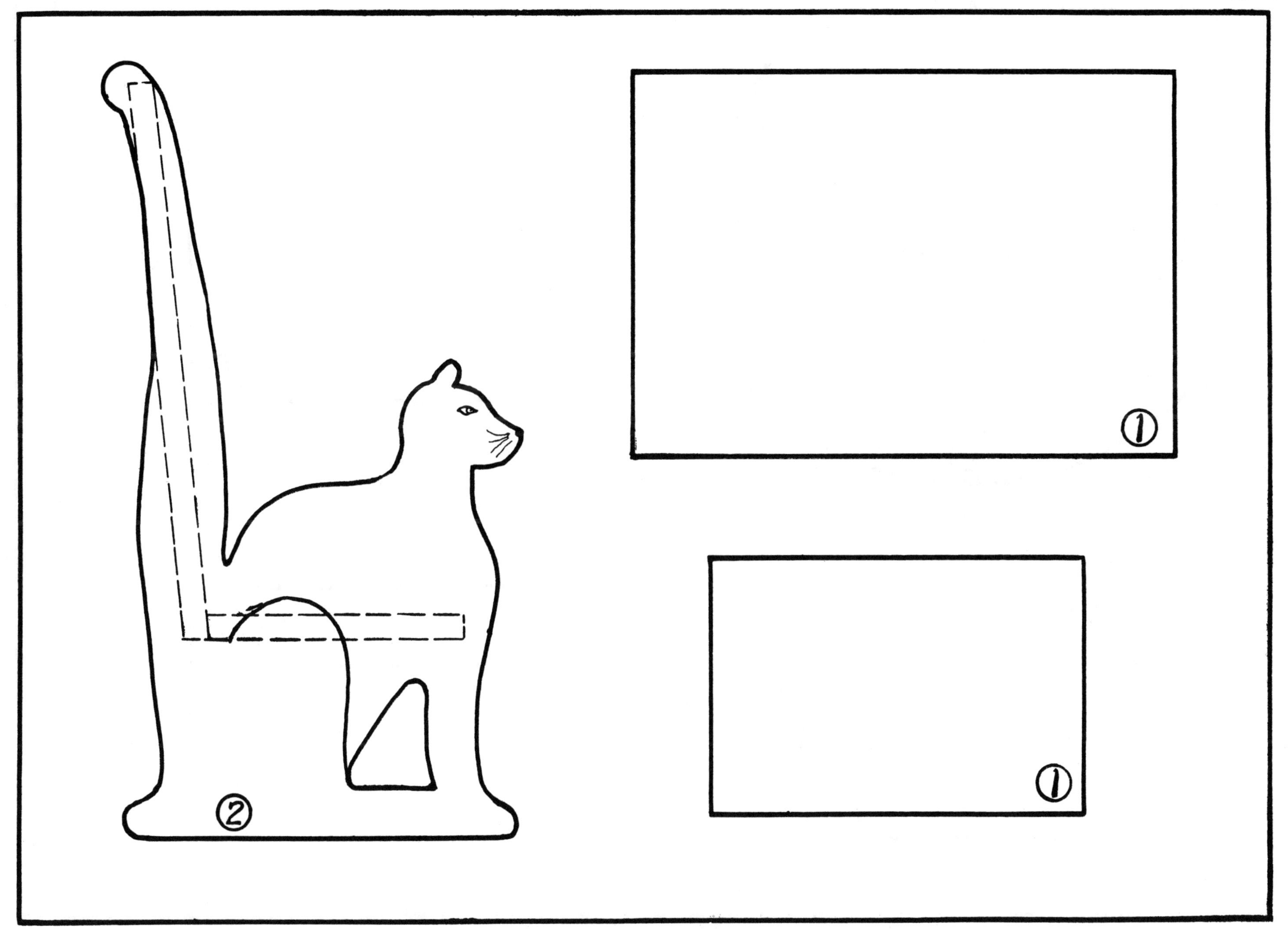

Plate 84—Patterns for Cat Chair.

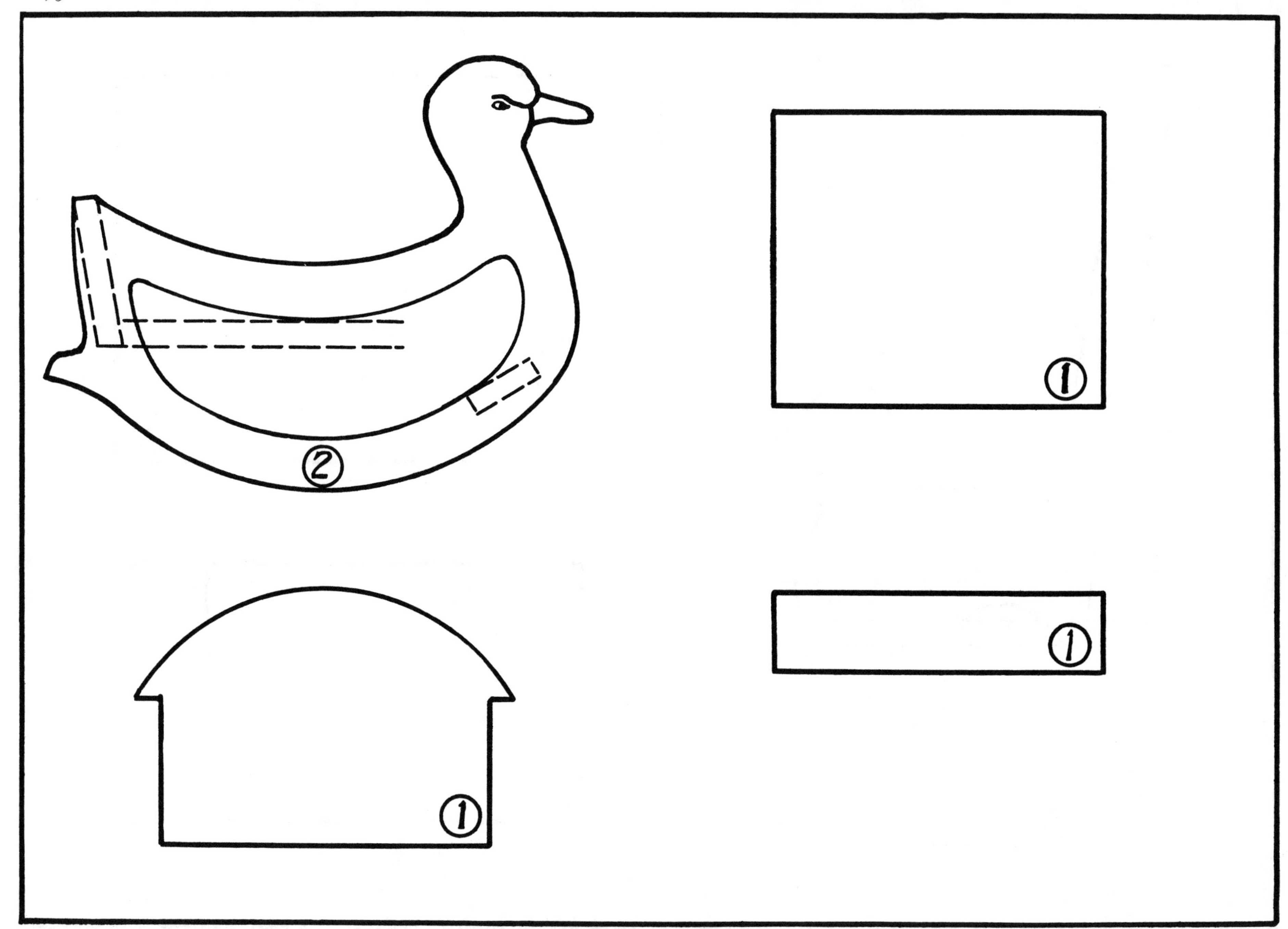

Plate 85—Patterns for Duck Rocker.

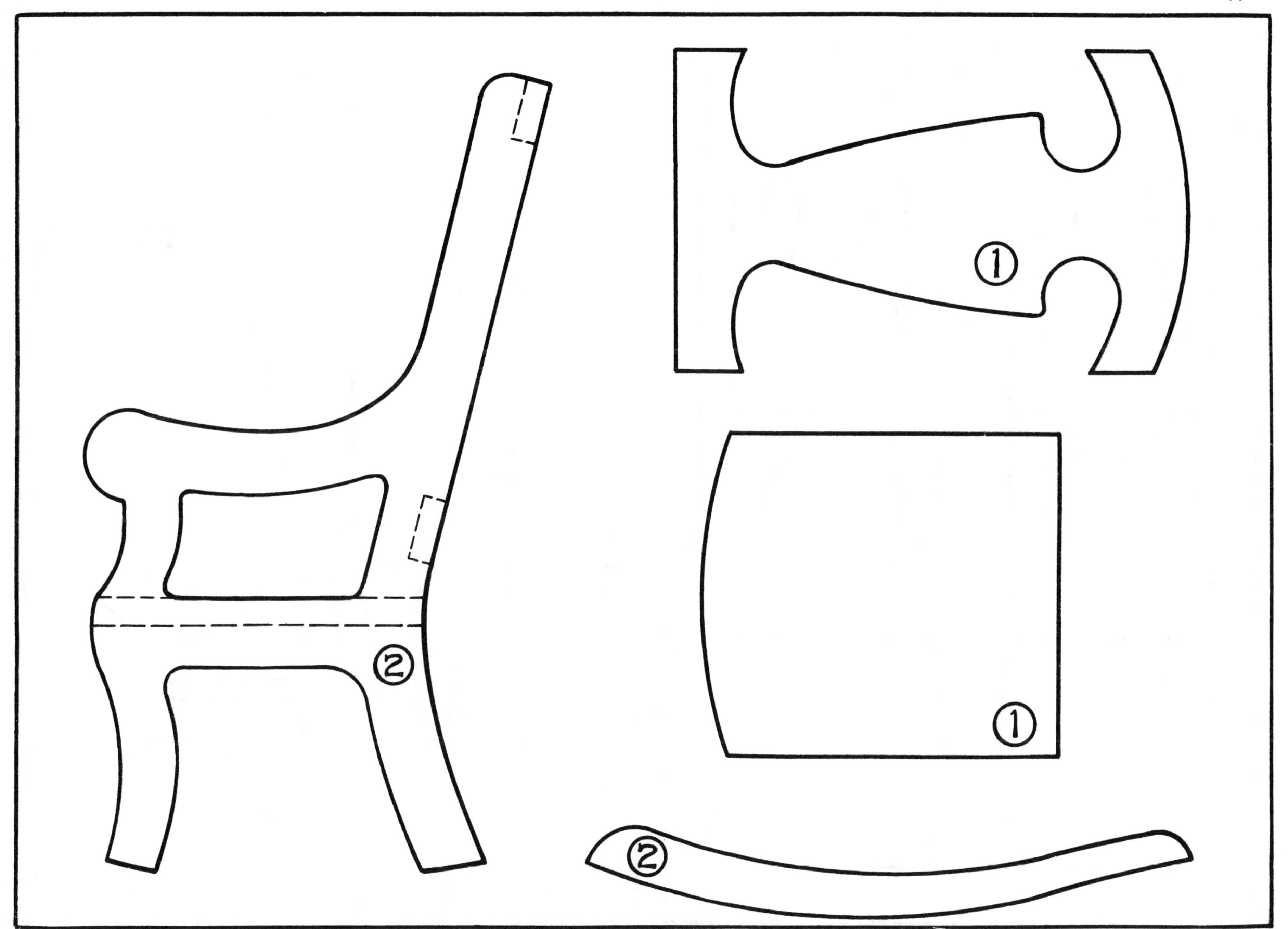

Plate 86—Patterns for Rocking-chair.

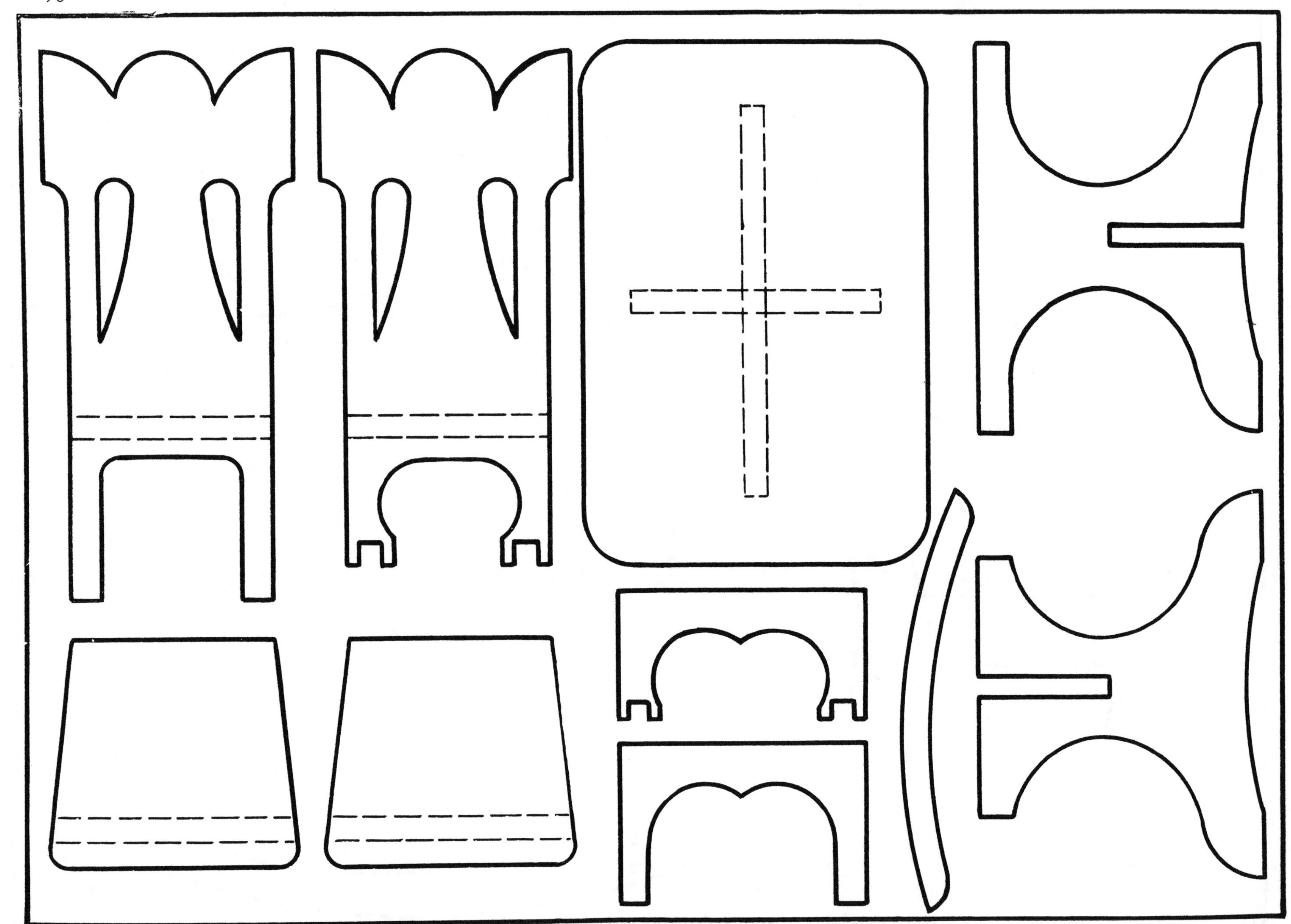

Plate 87—Patterns for Dining-Room Set.

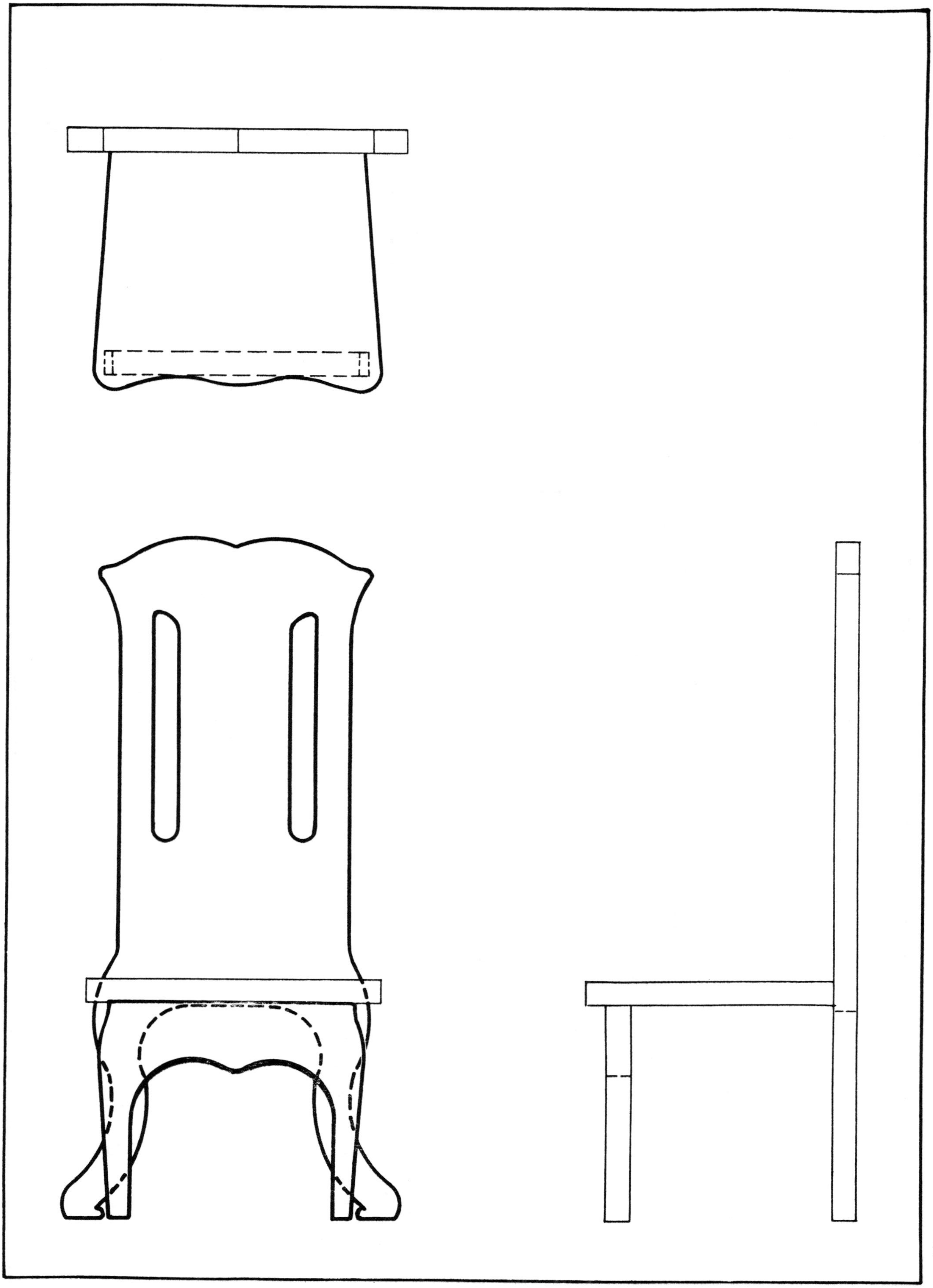

Plate 88—Pattern for Hall Chair.

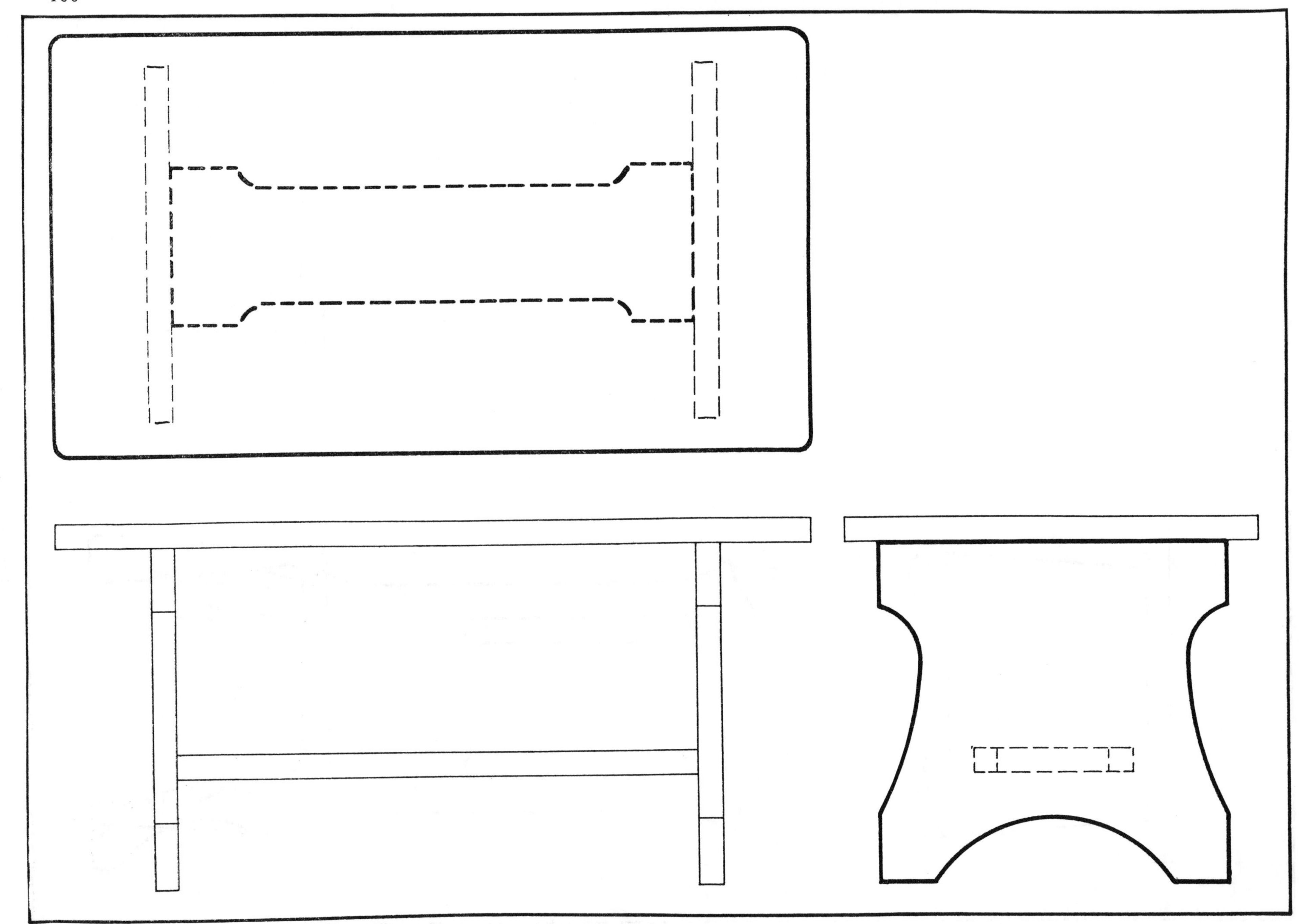

Plate 89—Pattern for Dining-Room Table.

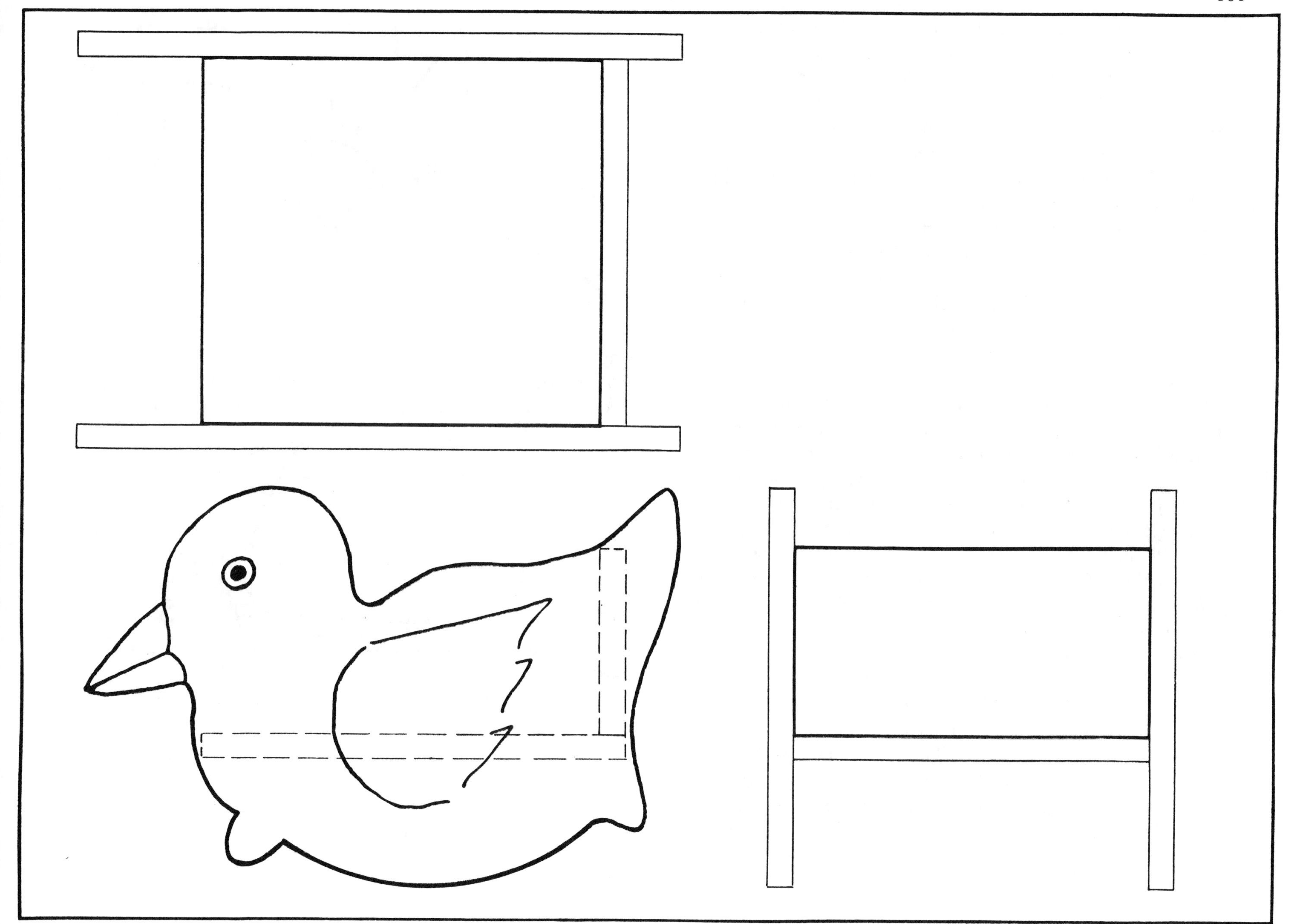

Plate 90—Pattern for Duck Rocking-chair.

spokes. In order to cut out the pieces, small holes are bored with the brad awl. The saw blade is removed from the saw frame, shoved through one of the holes, and then placed back into the frame. After the piece is sawed out, the saw blade is removed from the frame and the wheel slipped off. The rest of the construction is the same as in previous problems.

Plate 94 contains the patterns for the Chariot shown in the lower left-hand corner of Plate 91. A list of pieces not shown but needed is given with the patterns.

Plate 95 shows the patterns for the Sleigh in the lower right-hand corner of Plate 91. The patterns for all the pieces are given, except the bottom which is just a straight, flat, rectangular piece, 3 inches by 4¼ inches.

All the vehicles described should be well painted and shellacked.

Plate 96 shows a Toy Wagon constructed of light wood. Instead of giving the patterns of this toy, we have given in Plate 97 dimensioned details drawn to scale. Here the boy must lay out the work from the drawings with the rule, try-square, and compass. This will be a new experience for the boy, and with a little help from the teacher, it can easily be accomplished.

Plate 98 shows a toy Aeroplane which may be constructed by some of the older and more ambitious boys. The scale drawings for the parts are shown in Plate 99. By using a strong, wide, rubber band in connection with the propeller, as shown, this Aeroplane may be made to fly.

THE KICKING DONKEY

Plate 101 shows the various parts necessary for the construction of a Kicking Donkey. The lower half of Plate 100 illustrates the parts assembled. This is, without exception, one of the most interesting of the mechanical toys. The clown is very loosely jointed and fastened to the donkey's back with a long cotter pin. A string is tied to the donkey's nose and brought through a small brass ring fastened to the base, or through a hole in the base. When the string is pulled, the

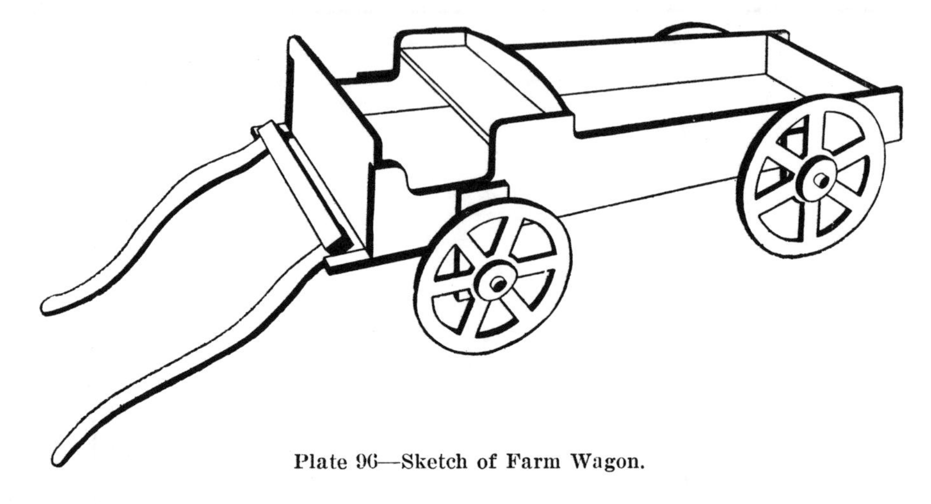

Plate 96—Sketch of Farm Wagon.

Plate 98—Sketch of Aeroplane.

Plate 91—Sketches of Toy Vehicles.

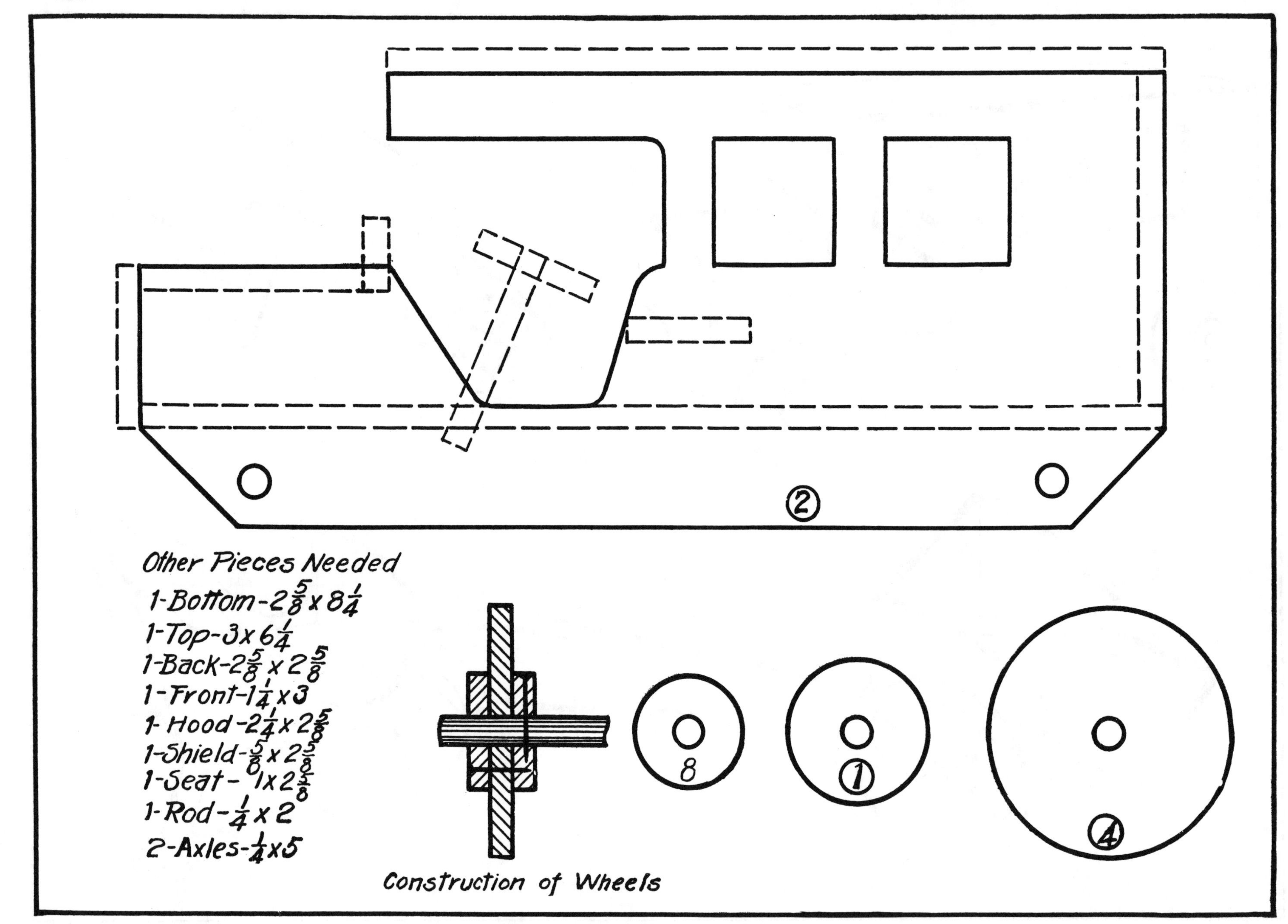

Plate 92—Patterns for Automobile Truck.

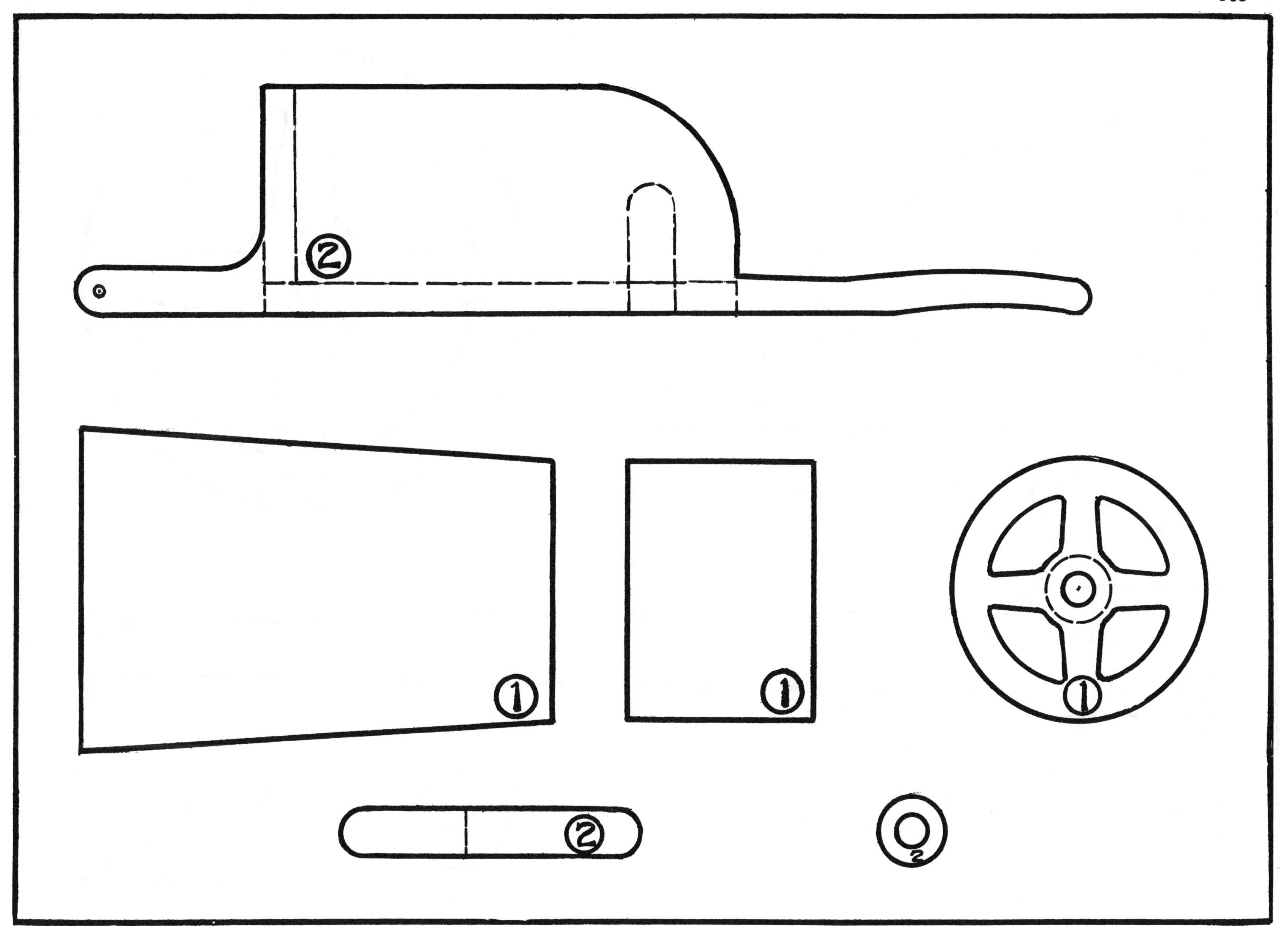

Plate 93—Patterns for Wheelbarrow.

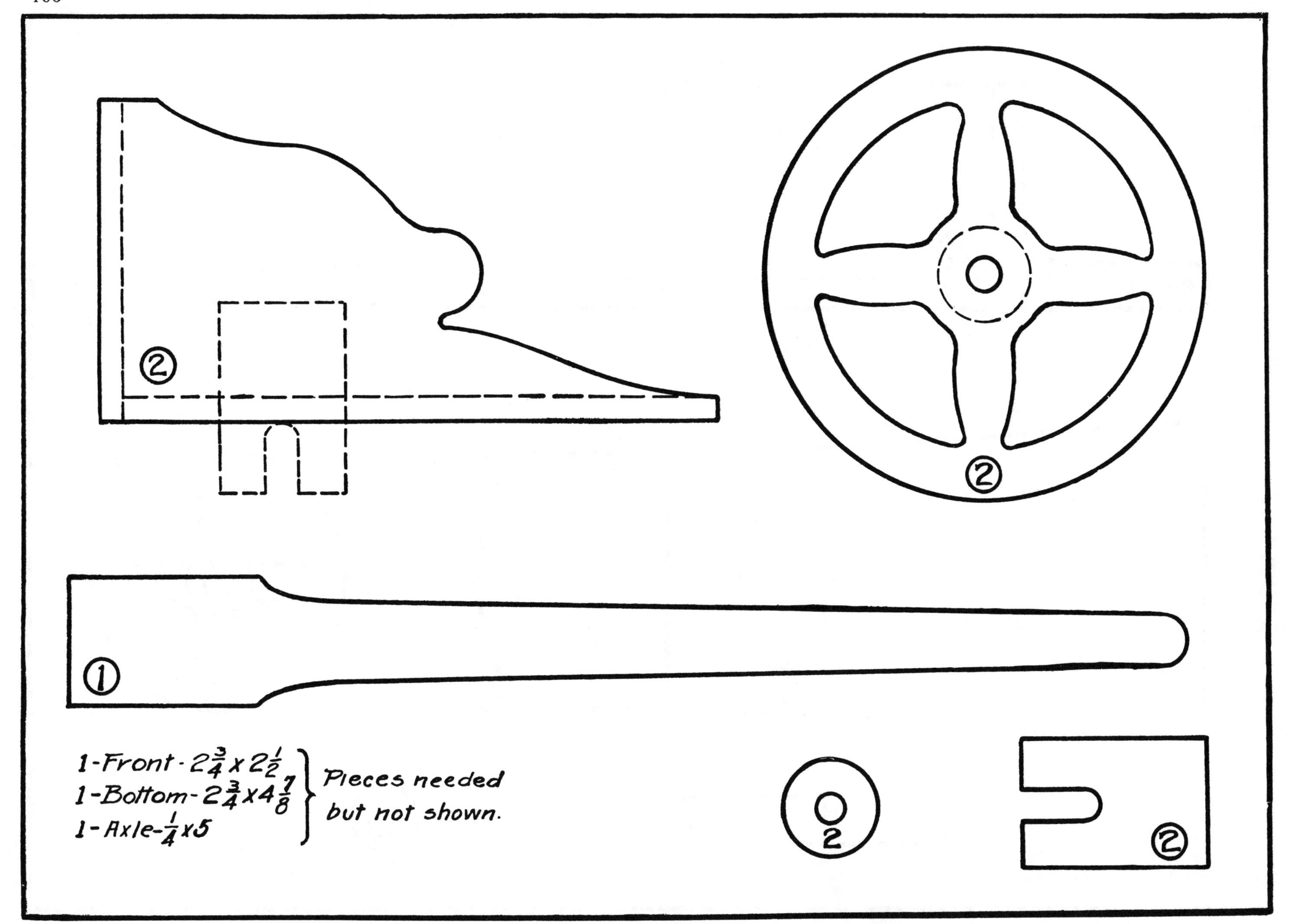

Plate 94—Patterns for Chariot.

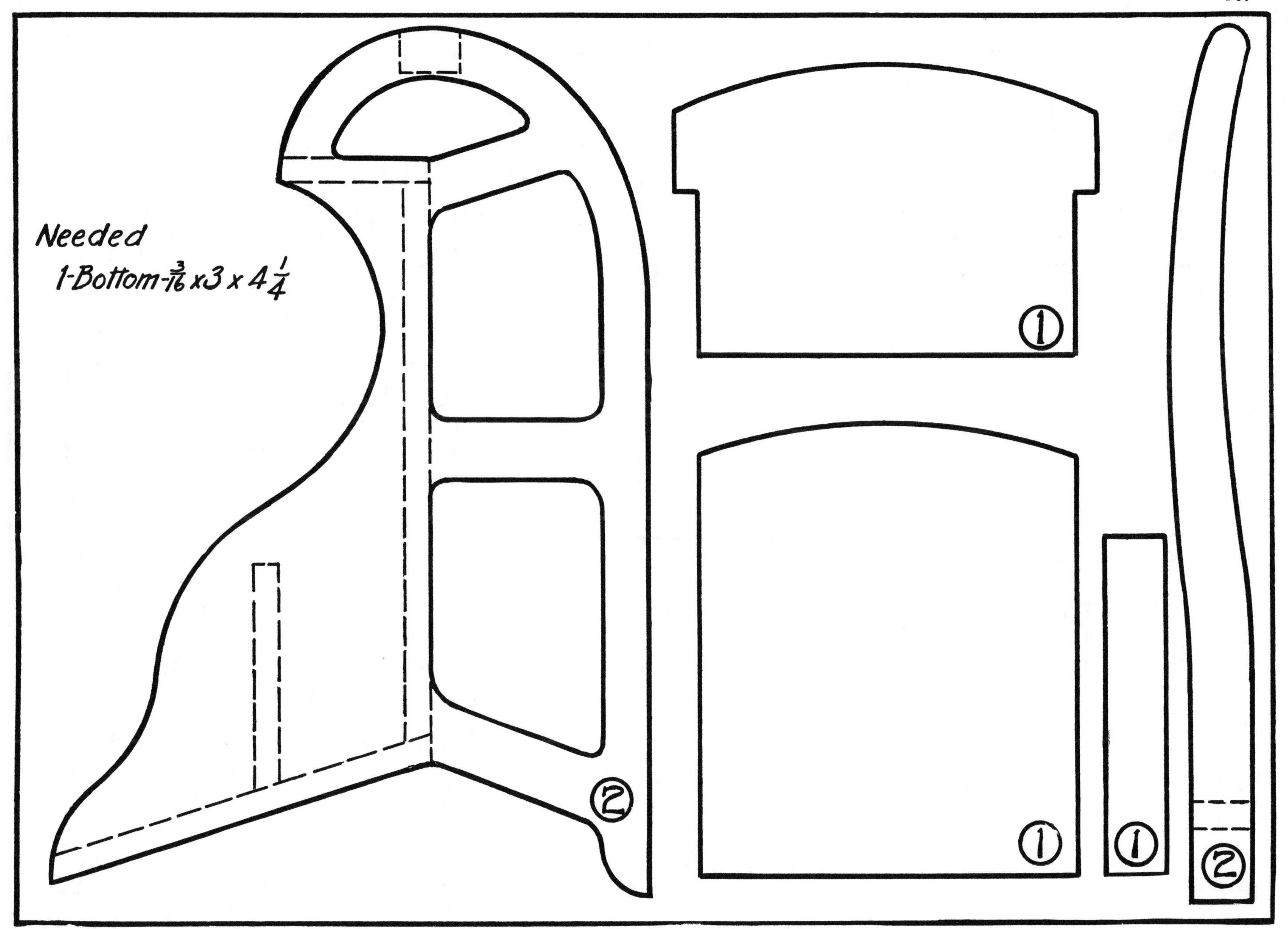

Plate 95—Patterns for Sleigh.

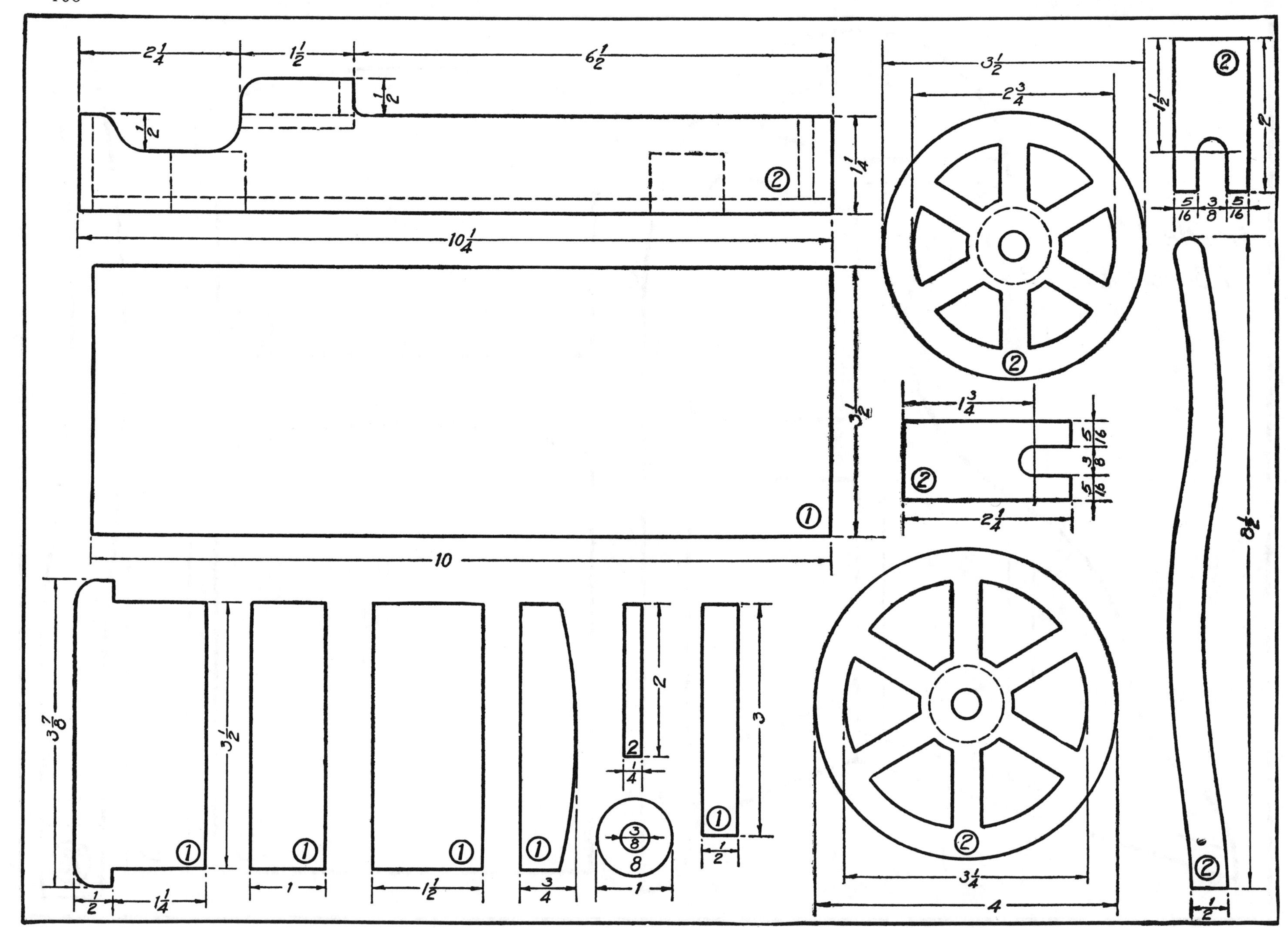

Plate 97—Detail Drawings of Farm Wagon.

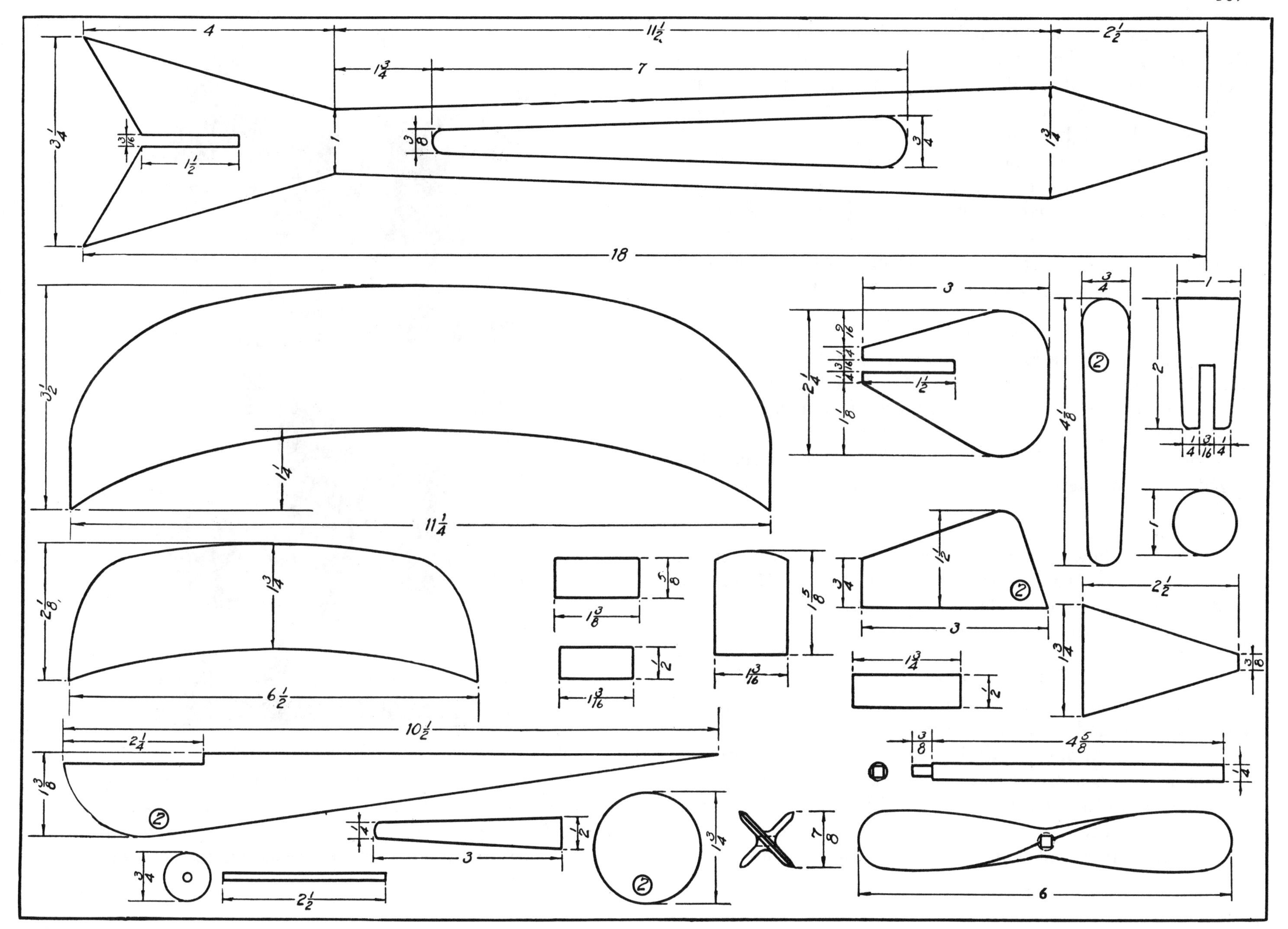

Plate 99—Detail Drawing of Aeroplane.

donkey kicks his hind legs and the clown is thrown forward. By allowing a rubber band to extend from between the hind legs to a small staple in the standard, the hind legs are drawn back in position when the pull on the string is released. The clown should be highly colored.

The upper half of Plate 100 shows another donkey that is capable of moving his tail and ears, when the string is pulled. Plate 102 shows the parts necessary, and Plate 100 shows the parts assembled. Unless the joints are very loose, the tail and ears will not return to their original position without additional weight. The dotted lines show the arrangement of the strings.

MATCH SAFES

Unique Match Safes may be constructed on flat, one-piece animal shapes, as shown in Plate 103. A small box is made and tacked to the animal shape. A piece of sandpaper is glued on the cover of the box. To set off the sandpaper a small border may be placed around it, as shown. The children should be urged to make original drawings for these flat shapes.

TOPS

Plate 104 shows several simple Tops which may be constructed from ordinary spools and dowel rods. A Disk Top, made of light wood and a dowel rod, is also shown.

Two forms of Buzzers also appear in this plate.

BIRD HOUSES

Every boy ought to know more about the characteristics and habits of birds and about the many ways in which they may be attracted to the farm or town-home grounds. It is known that certain uncivilized tribes have great facility in taming wild creatures, and often share their home with a variety of furred and feathered pets. We are told that primitive man had pets, among them birds, and that without doubt he provided nesting

Plate 105.

facilities for some birds. It is said that the early colonists of North America found that some agricultural tribes of eastern Indians hung up gourds for purple martins, on trees trimmed to bare poles. How old the practice is, we have no means of

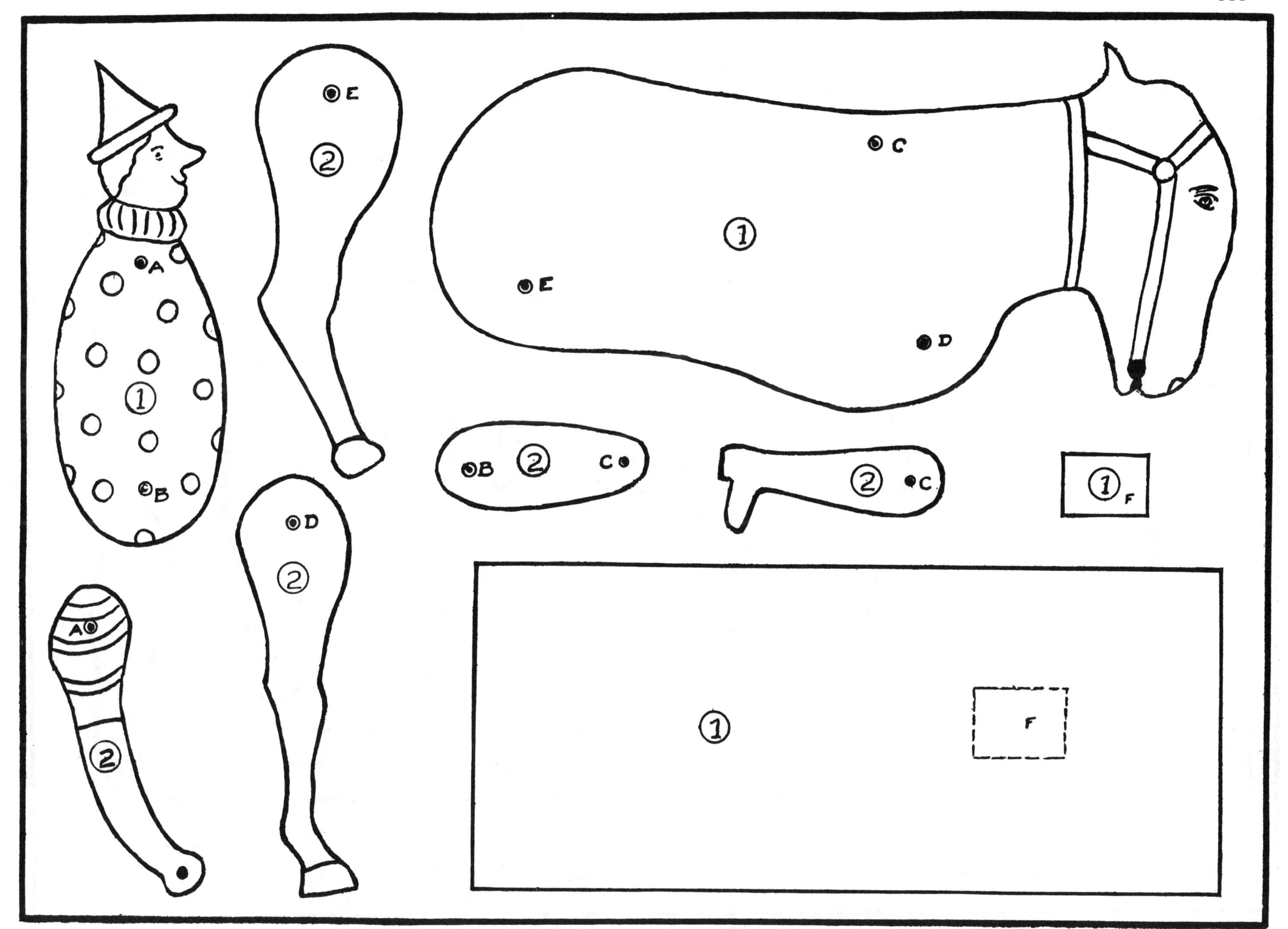

Plate 101—Detail Parts for Clown and Donkey.

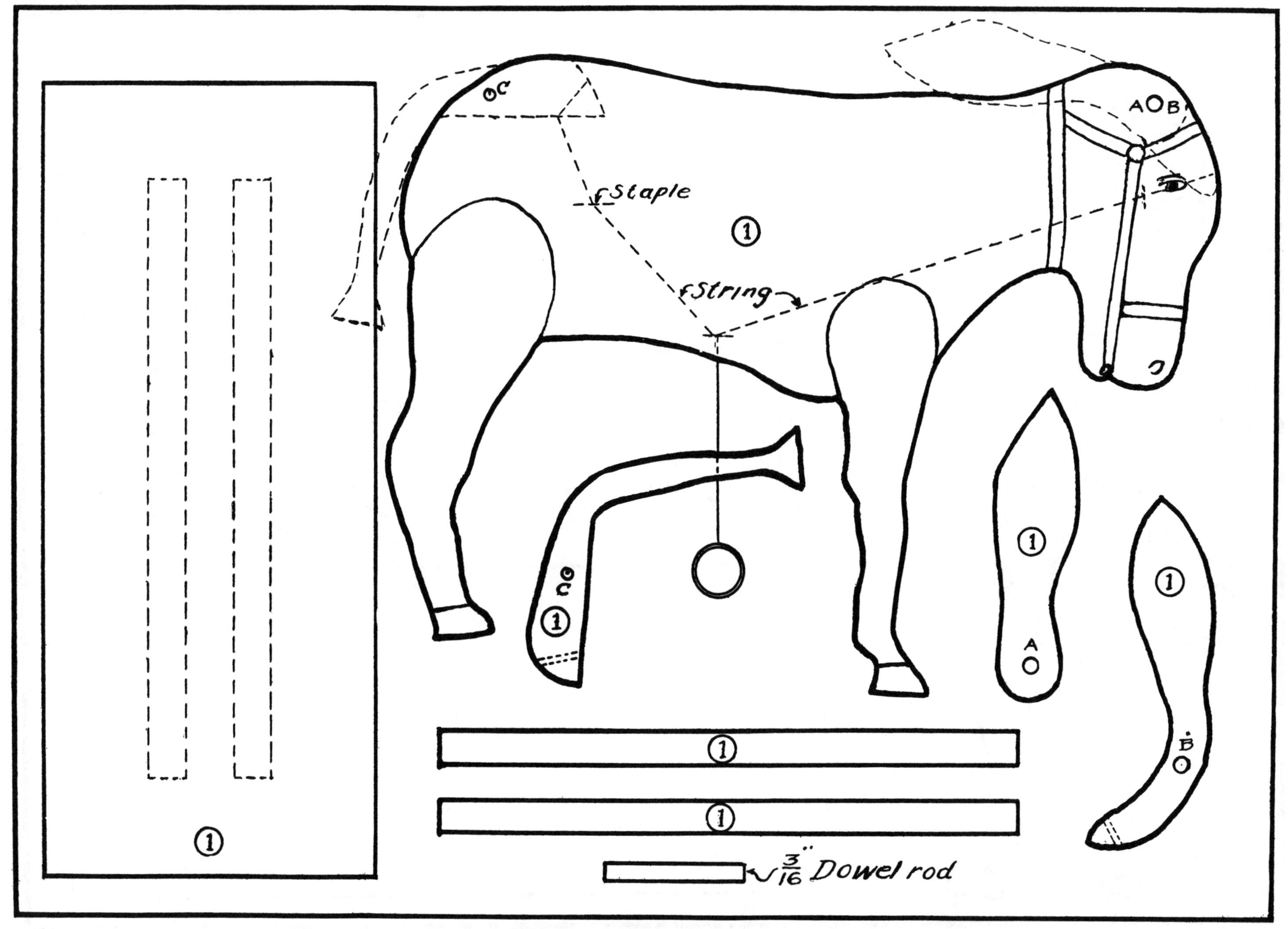

Plate 102—Detail Parts for Donkey.

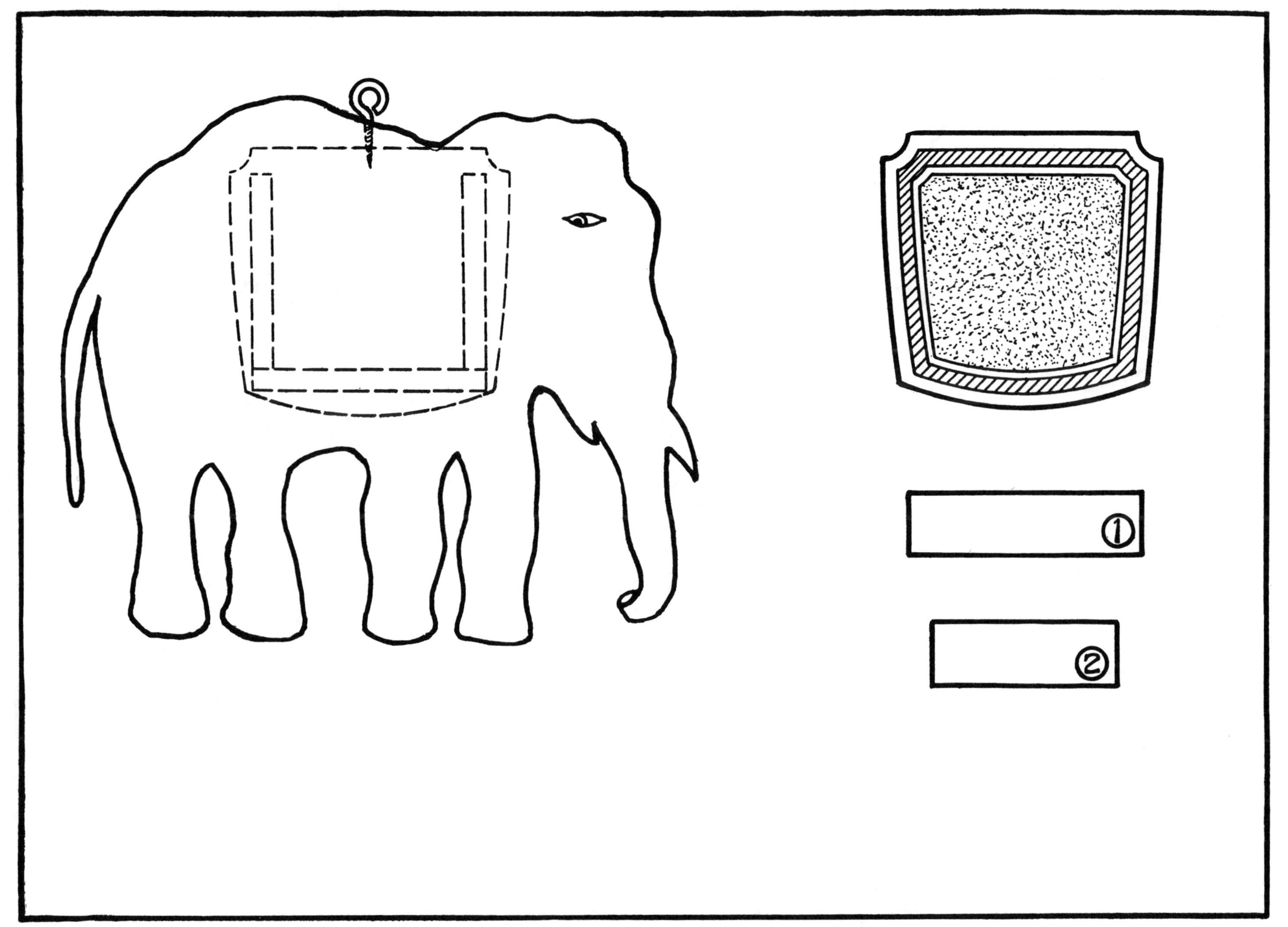

Plate 103—Patterns for Match Holder.

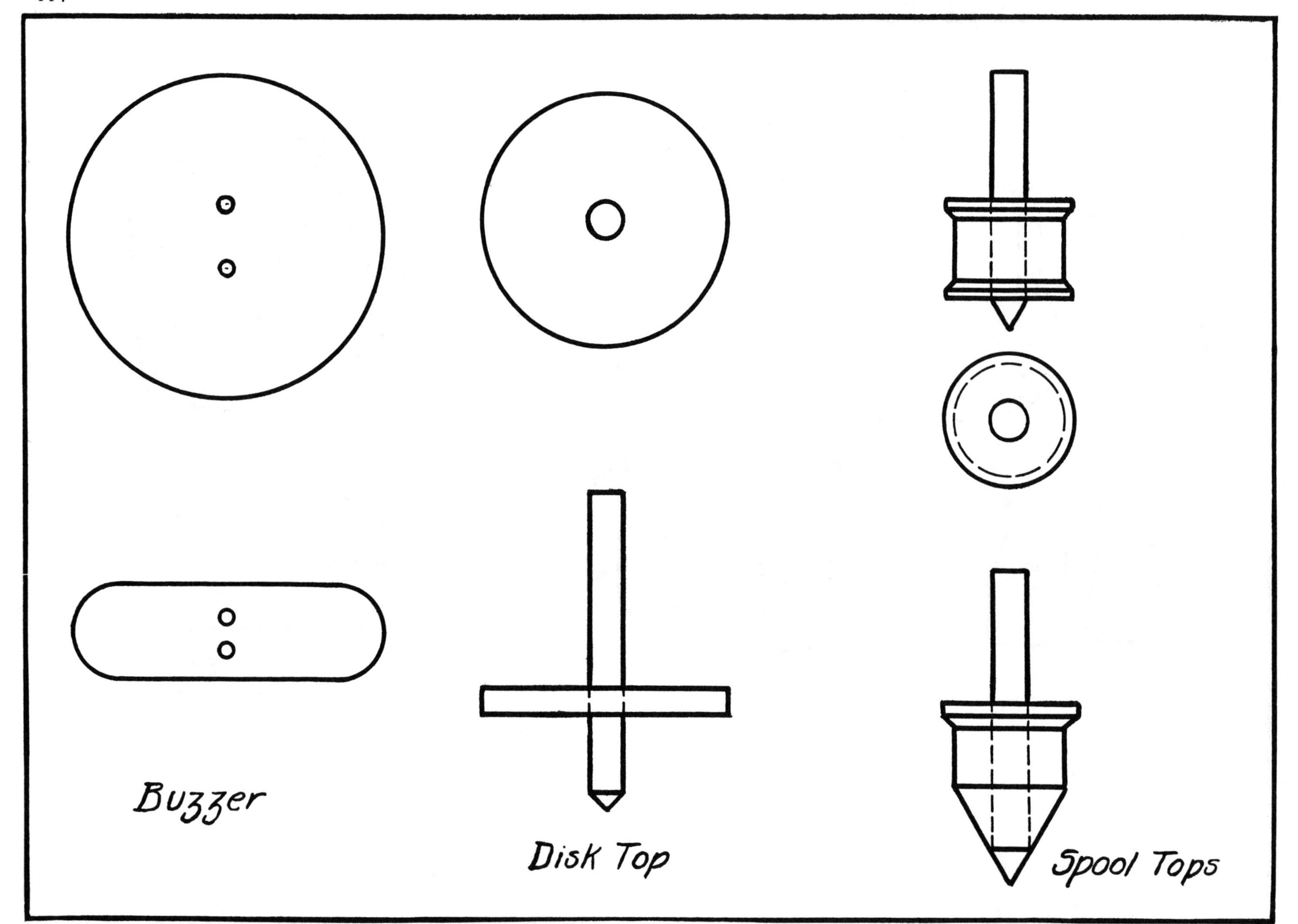

Plate 104—Toy Tops and Buzzer.

knowing, but it has been continued by white men to this day, in but slightly modified form, throughout the southern states.

Every farmer and forester of this country should know more about birds. It has been stated that the loss to cereal crops through insect pests amounts annually to $200,-000,000. According to statistics of the U. S. Department of Agriculture, the cotton growers alone lose $60,000,000 a year and the timber interests $100,000,000, through insect pests. Birds would aid greatly in doing away with much of this great loss if farmers and others give them a chance.

It is estimated that each insectivorous bird will consume 100 insects a day. The stomach of a female martin has been found to contain more than 2,000 mosquitoes, a large number of house flies, cucumber beetles, and other insects. One pair of brown thrashers will destroy 50,000 insects in a single season.

If figures mean anything to the general public, the economic value of insectivorous birds can readily be appreciated. Their aesthetic value is beyond estimate. Man, who should be their greatest friend and protector, because he is their greatest benefactor, is in reality their worst enemy because of his ignorance.

With this valuable information at hand, it is clear that every one should make an effort not only to build attractive bird houses, but to make every effort to protect the birds from destroying agencies.

WREN HOUSE

Plates 105, 106, and 107 show plans for Wren Houses which are simple in construction. The parts may be cut with a coping saw. Care should be exercised in following the drawings, especially in making the hole for admitting the bird. If this is not adhered to, the larger birds, will drive away the smaller ones. The English sparrow and the wren are especially unwelcome tenants of houses planned for smaller birds.

CHICKADEE HOUSE

The chickadee is a bird quite worth while. A single chickadee will eat 400 insects, or up to 4,000 insect or worm eggs a day. Plate 108 shows a simple chickadee house.

TITMOUSE OR NUTHATCH HOUSE

The titmouse and nuthatch are among the most beneficial birds. It is said that an orchard ravaged by the codling worm can be virtually freed of this pest, if suet cages are placed to attract and keep nuthatches, chickadees, and downies in the neighborhood through the winter. Plate 109 shows a plan for housing these little creatures.

ROBIN SHELTER OR SHELF

The robin, perhaps the most domesticated of birds, will not build his nest in a house. For this reason the drawing of a shelf for robins is given in Plate 110. With the use of bark and twigs, the robin shelter may be made very rustic and most attractive to the birds. One side of the shelter is left open.

BLUEBIRD HOUSE

The Bluebird has become almost extinct in some sections of the United States. It is difficult to know just why this condition exists, but better bird house construction will do much to induce the few bluebirds we do have, to remain. See Plate 111.

KITES

Every boy, at certain seasons of the year, enjoys making and flying a kite. Excellent opportunity is offered in kitemaking for sawing strips of 3/16 inch or ⅜ inch bass wood. Plates 112 to 121 illustrate various types of kites and afford suggestions for interesting variations and original designs. Each plate contains sufficient dimensions so that written instructions are not necessary.

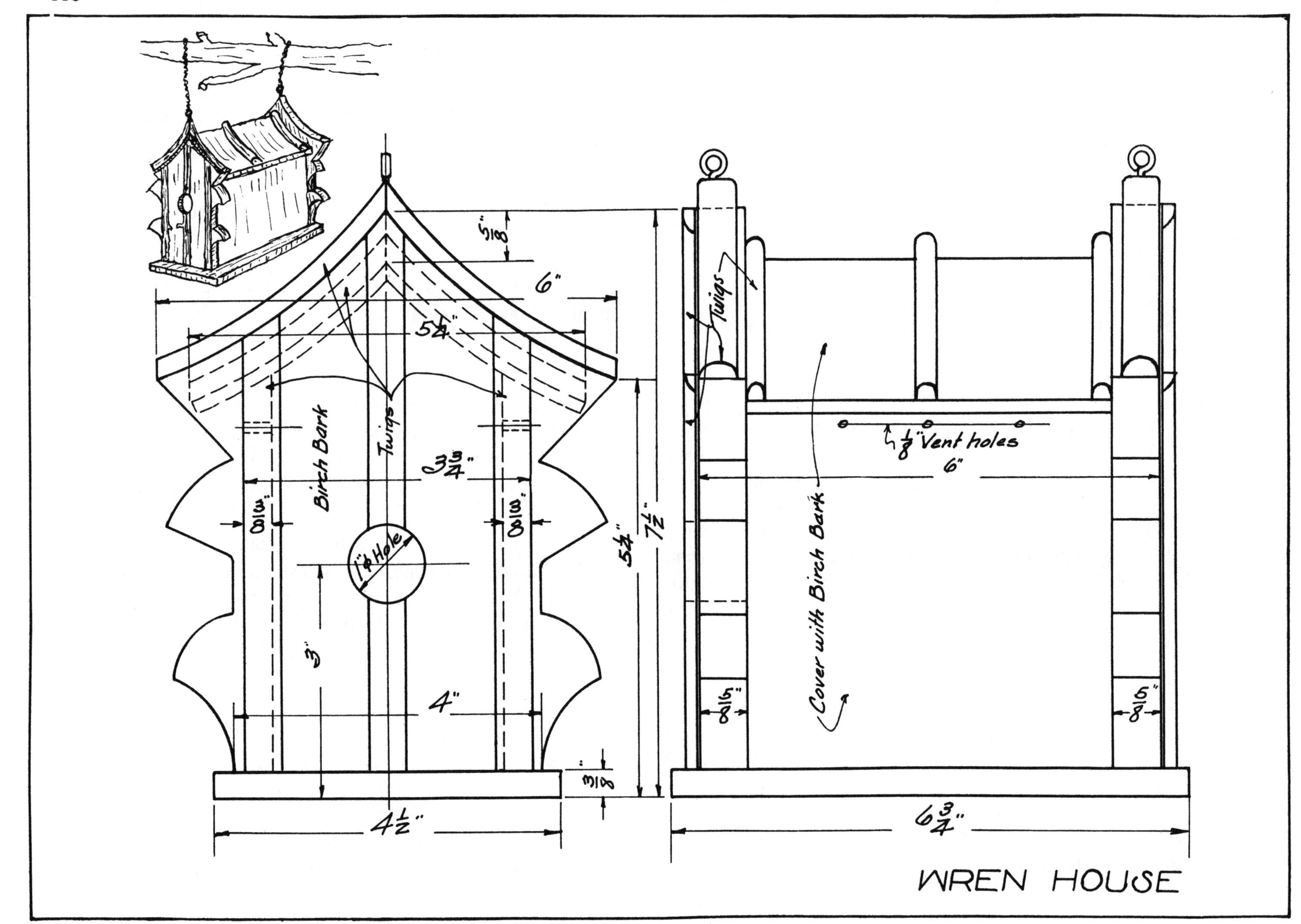
6"
5¼"
Twigs
Birch Bark
Twigs
3¾"
1¼ Hole
3"
4"
5¼"
7½"
4½"
Twigs
Cover with Birch Bark
⅛" Vent holes
6"
6¾"
WREN HOUSE

Plate 105.

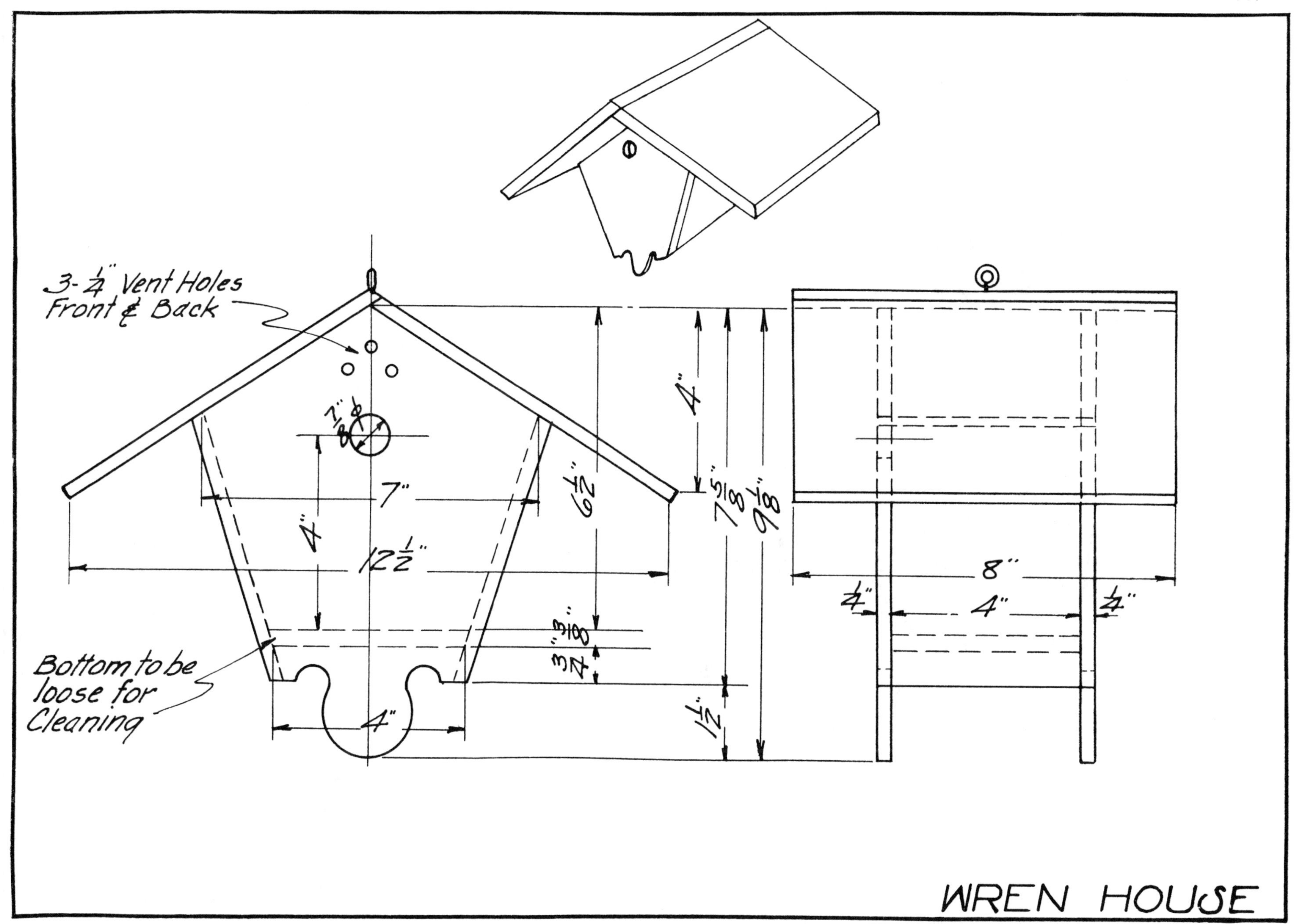
3-¼" Vent Holes Front & Back
7/8"
7"
4"
12½"
6½"
4"
7 5/8"
9 1/8"
3/8"
¾"
1½"
4"
Bottom to be loose for Cleaning
8"
¼"
4"
¼"
WREN HOUSE

Plate 106.

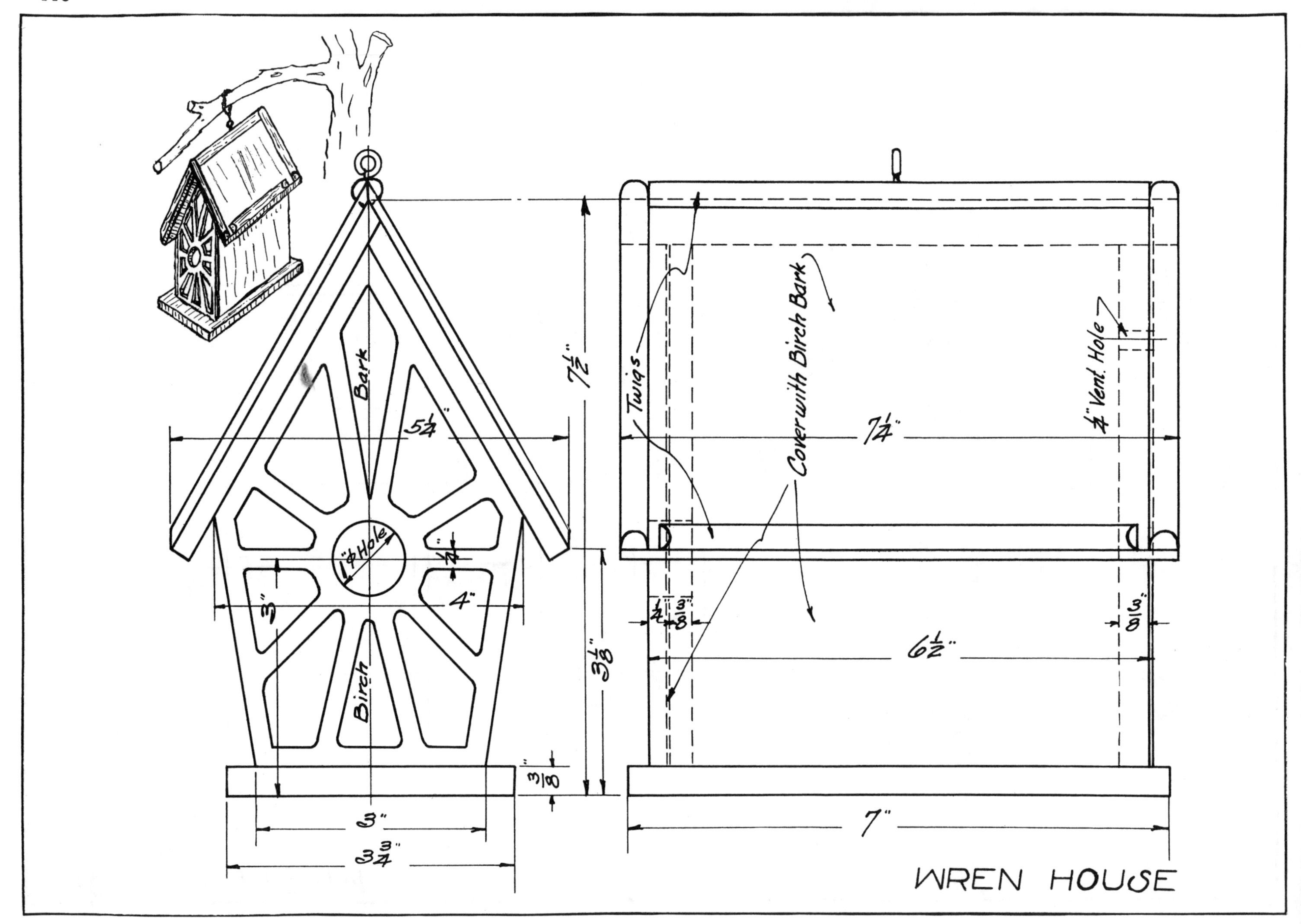

Bark
Birch
1"φ Hole
5¼"
7½"
3"
4"
¼"
3⅛"
3⅜"
3"
3¾"
Twigs
Cover with Birch Bark
¼" Vent. Hole
7¼"
¼"
⅜"
⅜"
6½"
7"
WREN HOUSE

Plate 107.

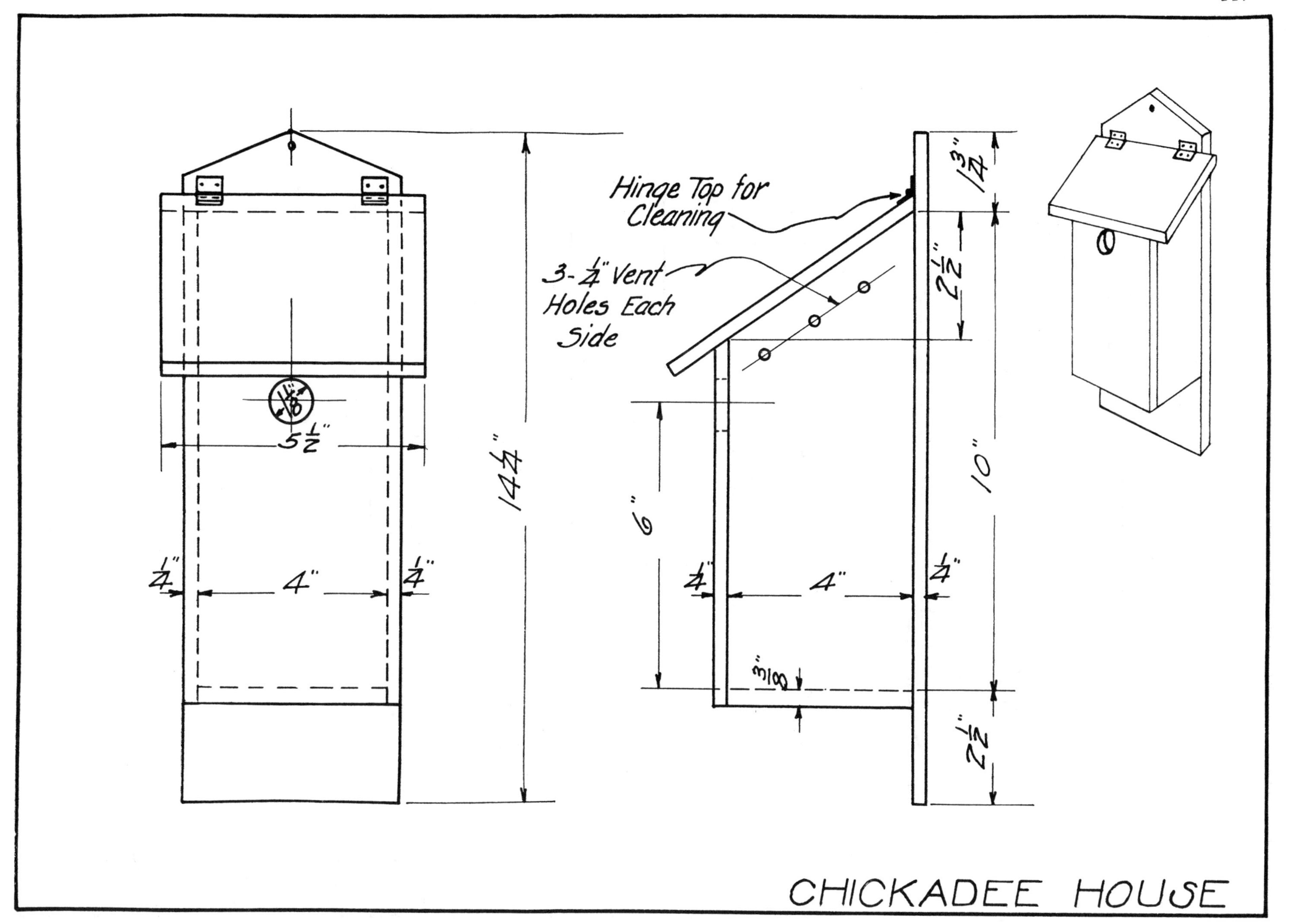
Hinge Top for Cleaning
3-1/4" Vent Holes Each Side
5 1/2"
14 1/4"
1/4"
4"
1/4"
1 3/4"
2 1/2"
10"
6"
3/8"
2 1/2"
CHICKADEE HOUSE

Plate 108.

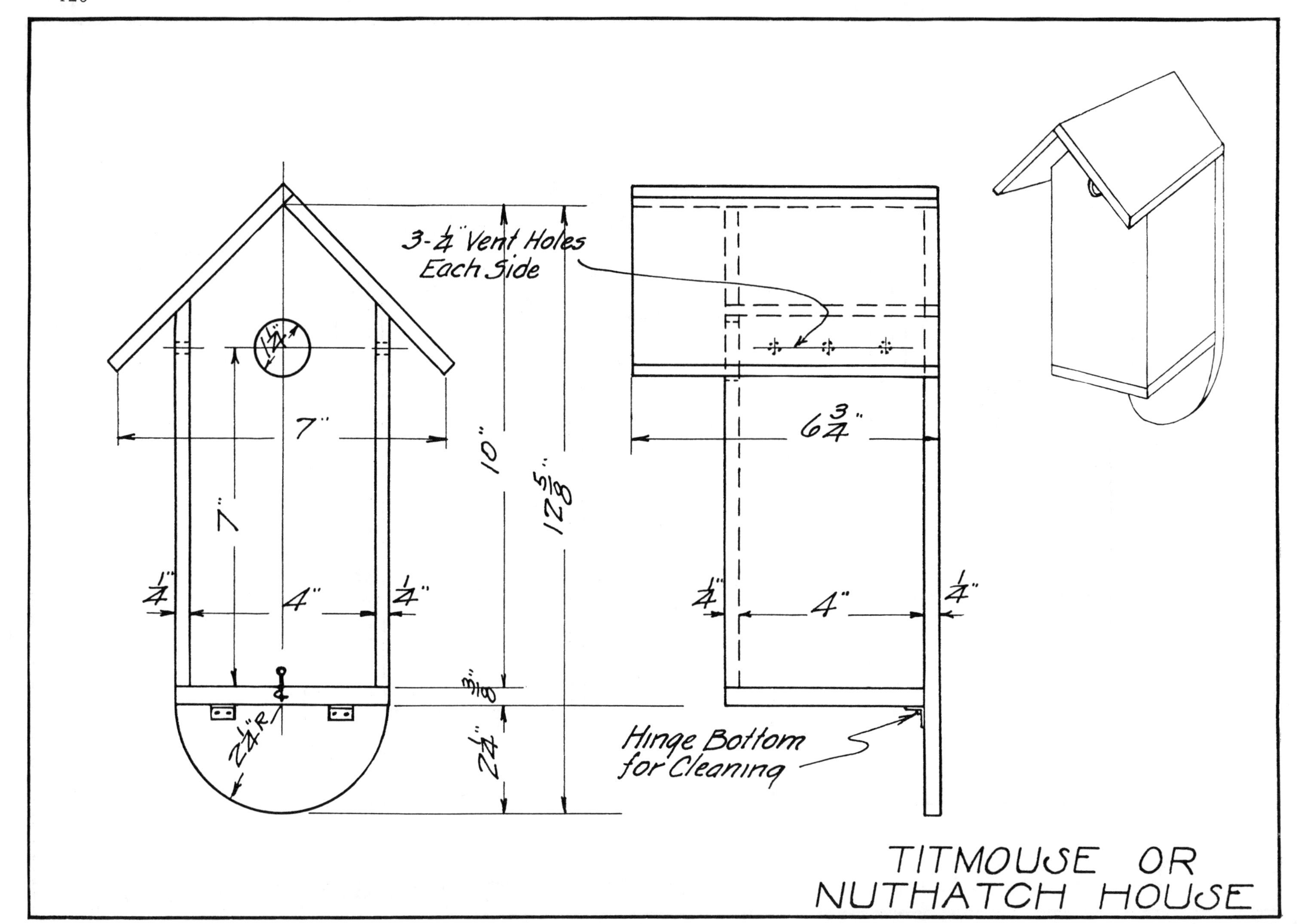
3-1/4" Vent Holes
Each Side
1 1/4"
7"
10"
12 5/8"
7"
1/4"
4"
1/4"
3/8"
2 1/4"R
2 1/4"
6 3/4"
1/4"
4"
1/4"
Hinge Bottom
for Cleaning
TITMOUSE OR
NUTHATCH HOUSE

Plate 109.

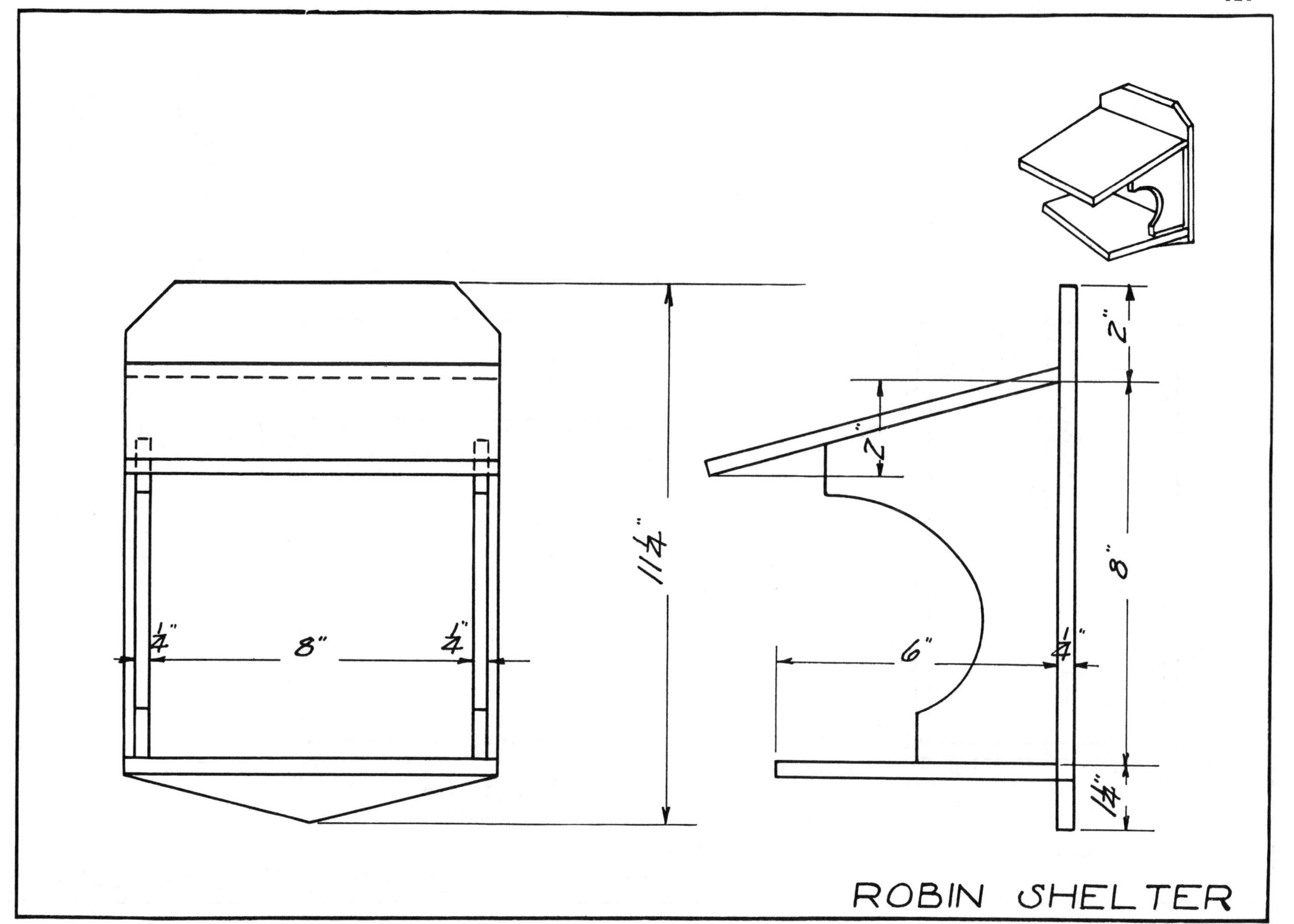

Plate 110.

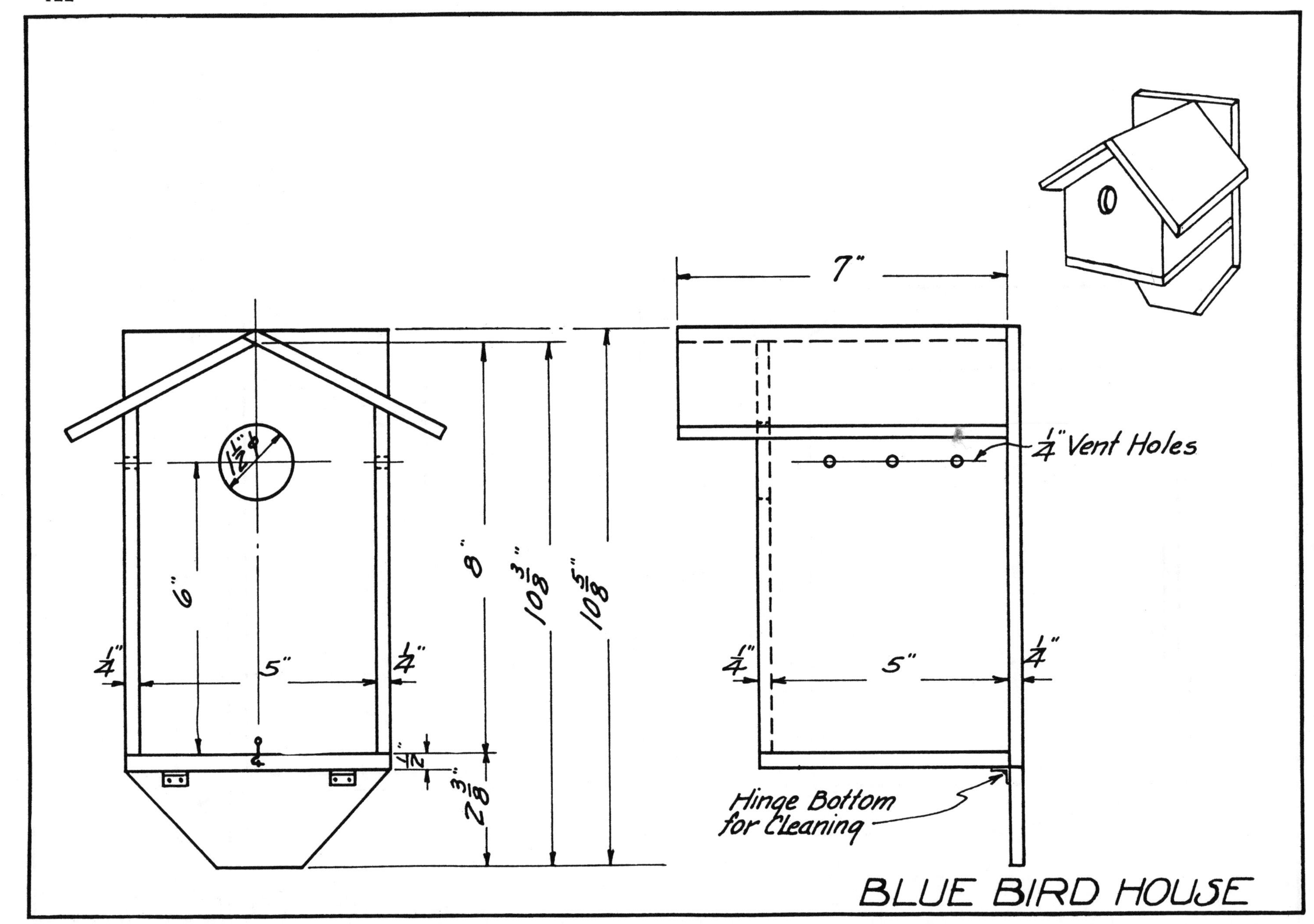
7"
1/4" Vent Holes
6"
8"
10 3/8"
10 5/8"
1/4"
5"
1/4"
1/2"
2 3/8"
Hinge Bottom
for Cleaning
BLUE BIRD HOUSE

Plate 111.

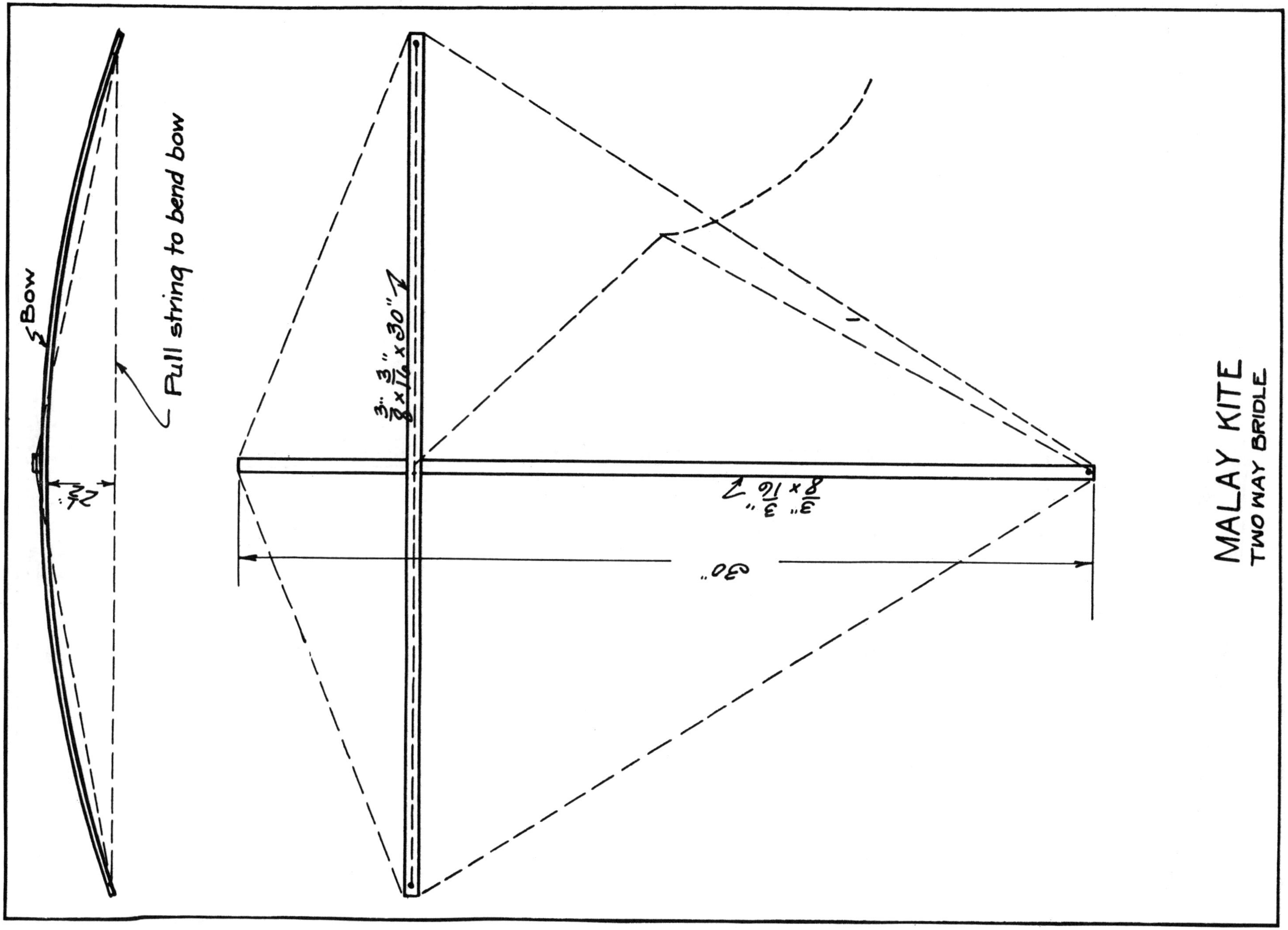

Bow
$2\frac{1}{2}$"
Pull string to bend bow
$\frac{3}{8}$" x $\frac{3}{16}$" x 30"
30"
$\frac{3}{8}$" x $\frac{3}{16}$"
MALAY KITE
TWO WAY BRIDLE

Plate 112.

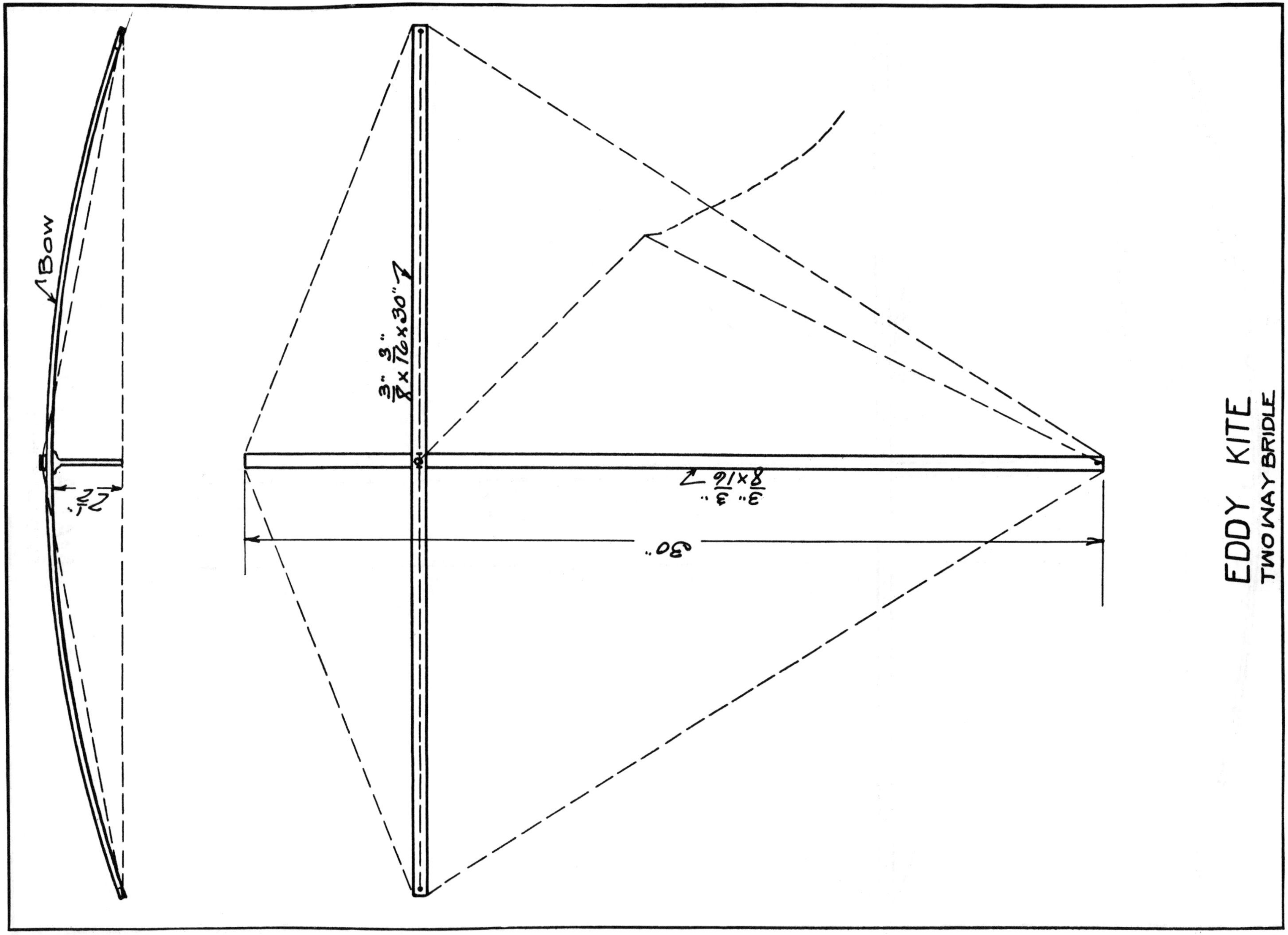

EDDY KITE

TWO WAY BRIDLE

Bow

$\frac{3}{8}$" x $\frac{3}{16}$" x 30"

$\frac{3}{8}$" x $\frac{3}{16}$"

30"

$2\frac{1}{2}$"

Plate 113.

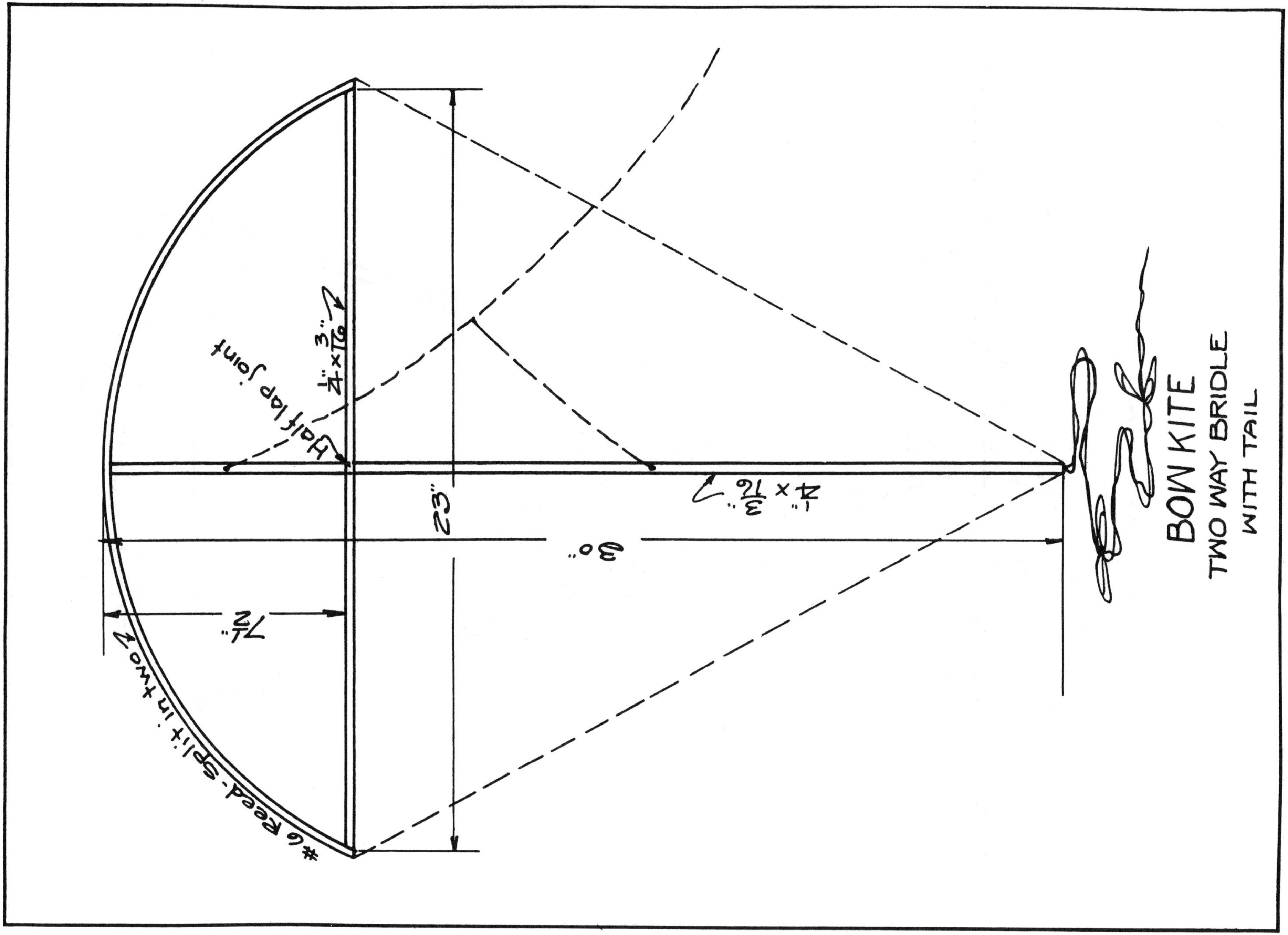

#6 Reed-Split in two

$7\frac{1}{2}$"

Half lap joint

$\frac{1}{4}$" x $\frac{3}{16}$"

23"

30"

$\frac{1}{4}$" x $\frac{3}{16}$"

BOW KITE

TWO WAY BRIDLE

WITH TAIL

Plate 114.

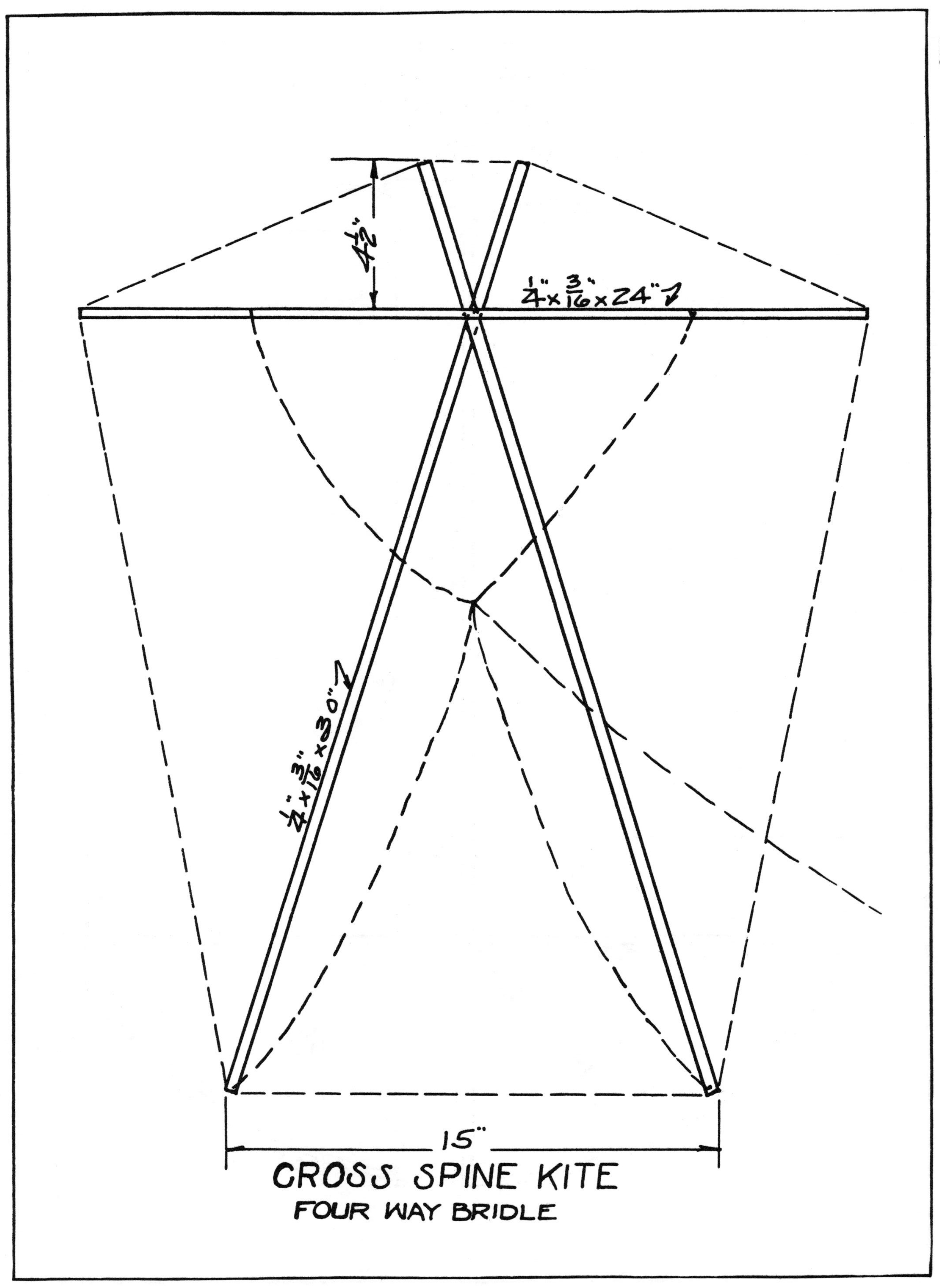

Plate 115.

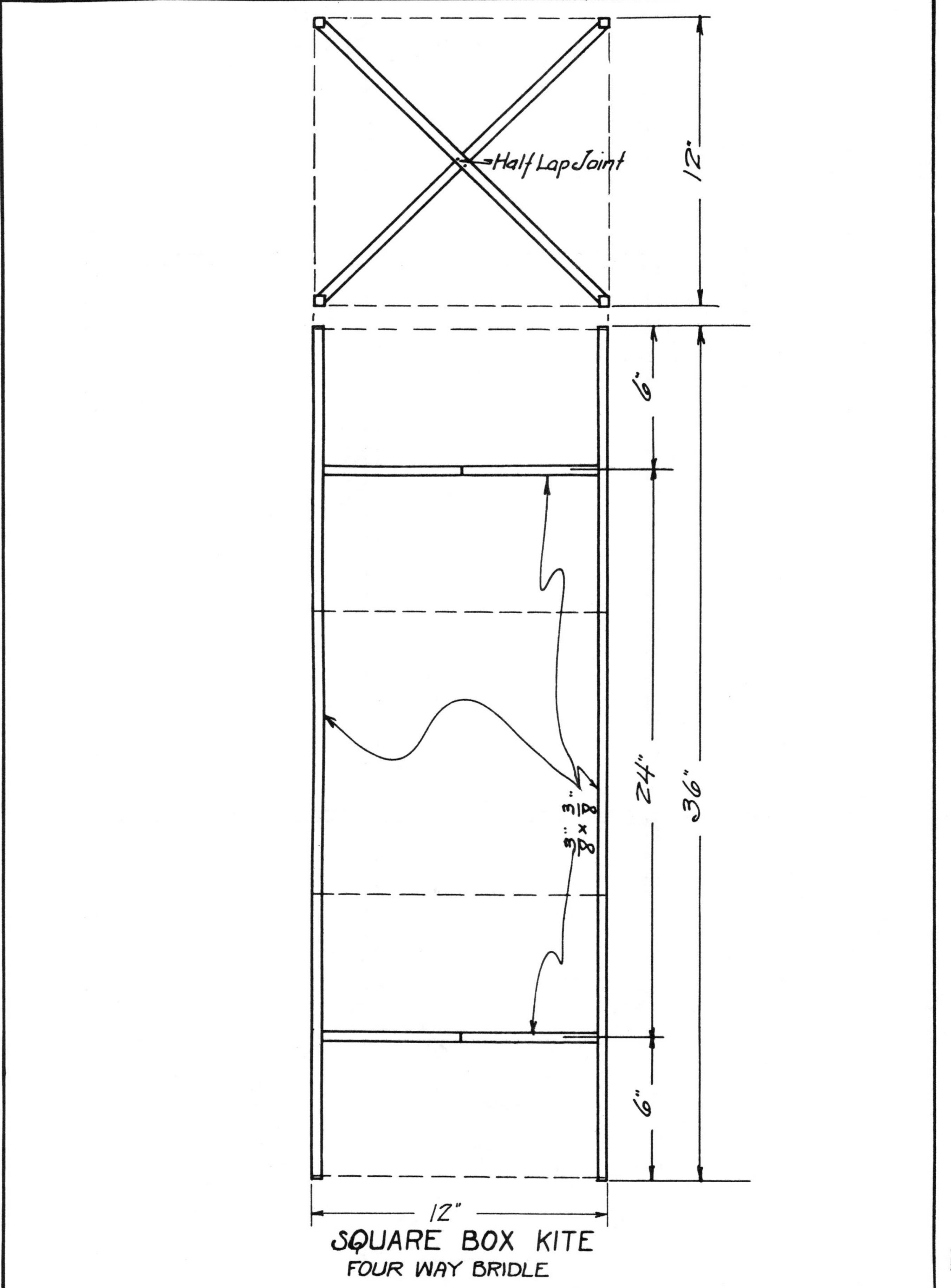
Half Lap Joint
12"
6"
24"
36"
3/8" x 3/8"
6"
12"
SQUARE BOX KITE
FOUR WAY BRIDLE

Plate 116.

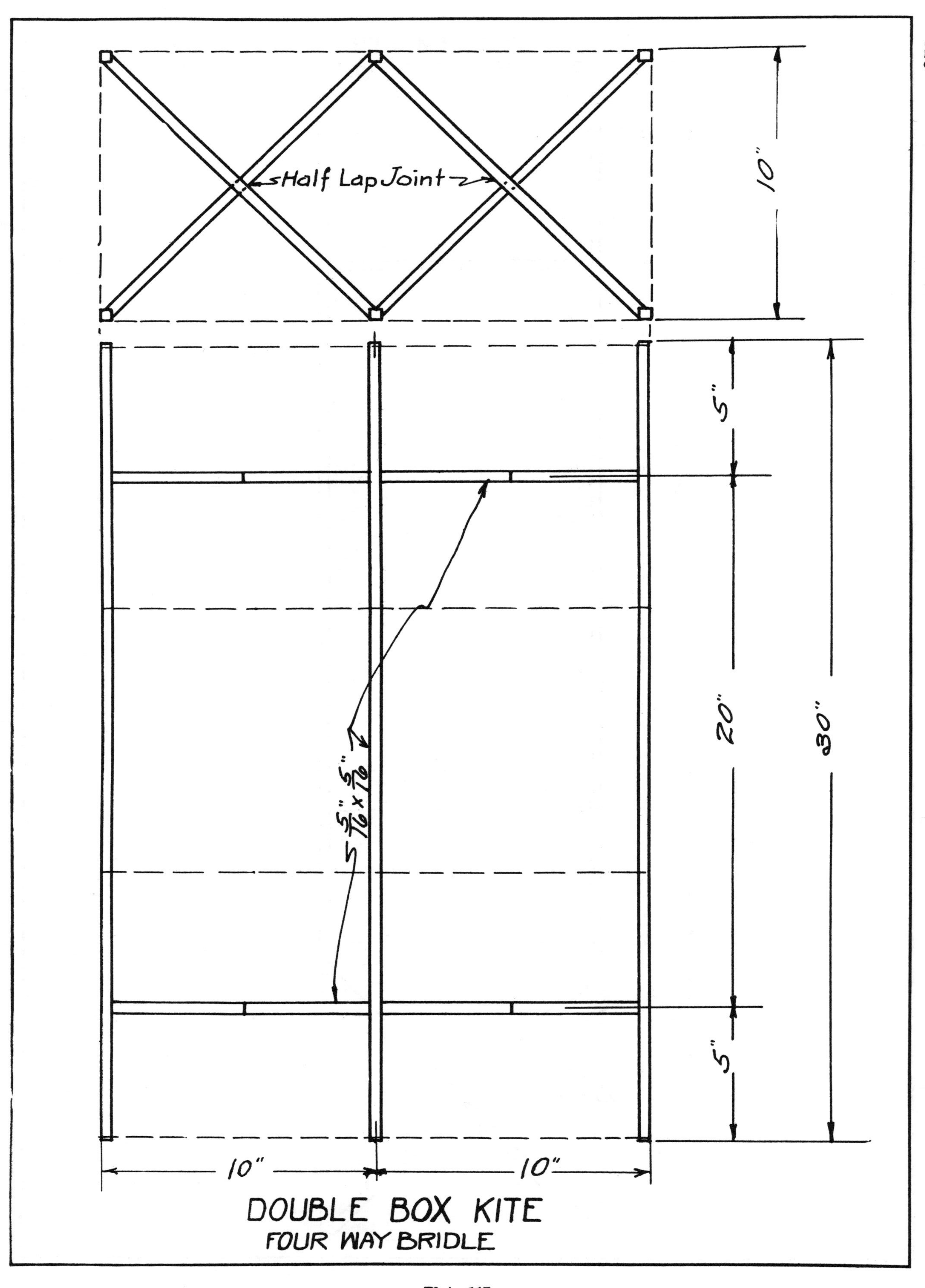
Half Lap Joint
10"
5"
20"
30"
5"
$\frac{5}{16}$" x $\frac{5}{16}$"
10"
10"
DOUBLE BOX KITE
FOUR WAY BRIDLE

Plate 117.

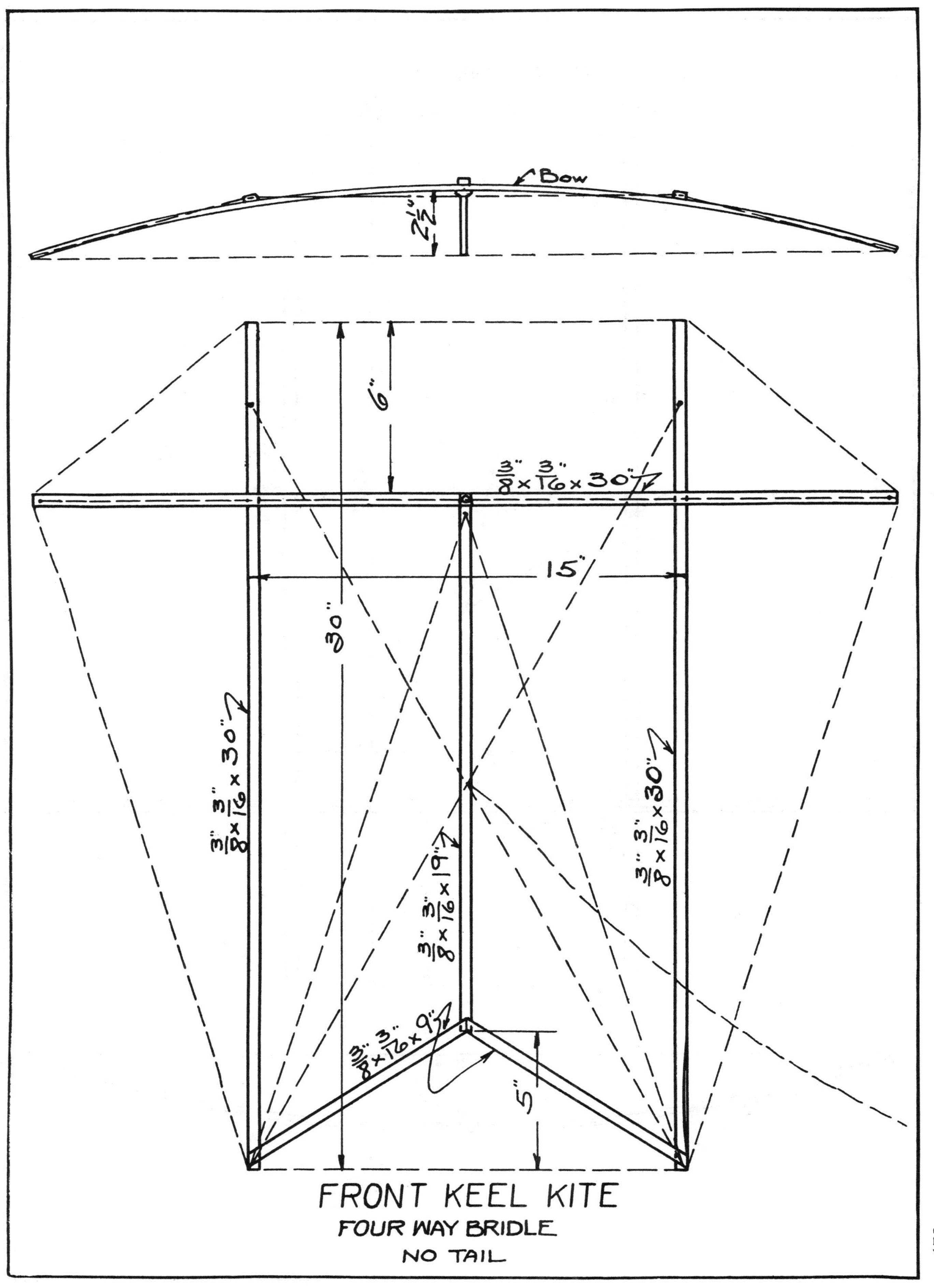
Bow
$2\frac{1}{2}$"
6"
$\frac{3}{8}$" × $\frac{3}{16}$" × 30"
15"
30"
$\frac{3}{8}$" × $\frac{3}{16}$" × 30"
$\frac{3}{8}$" × $\frac{3}{16}$" × 30"
$\frac{3}{8}$" × $\frac{3}{16}$" × 19"
$\frac{3}{8}$" × $\frac{3}{16}$" × 9"
5"
FRONT KEEL KITE
FOUR WAY BRIDLE
NO TAIL

Plate 118.

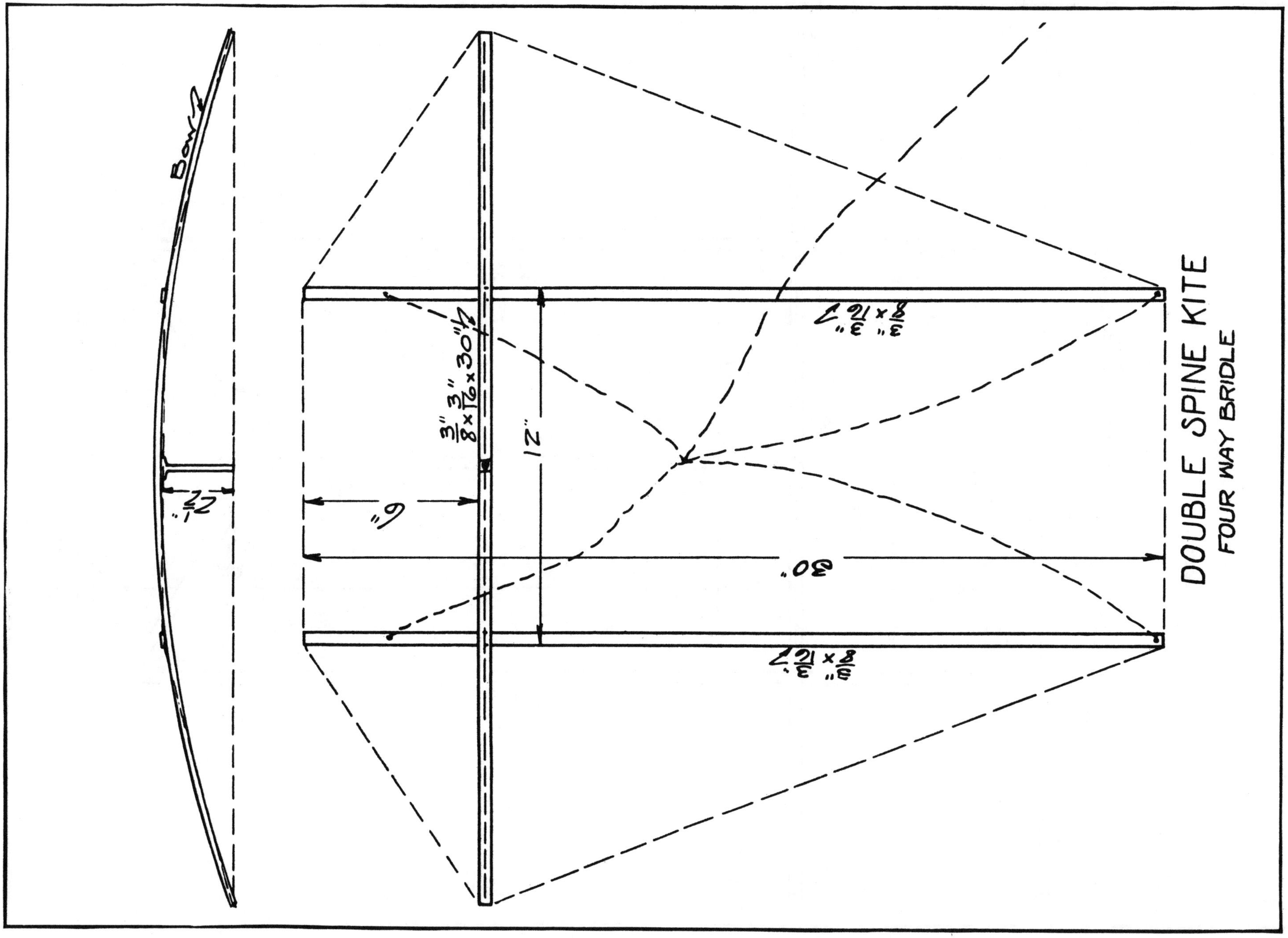

DOUBLE SPINE KITE
FOUR WAY BRIDLE

Plate 119.

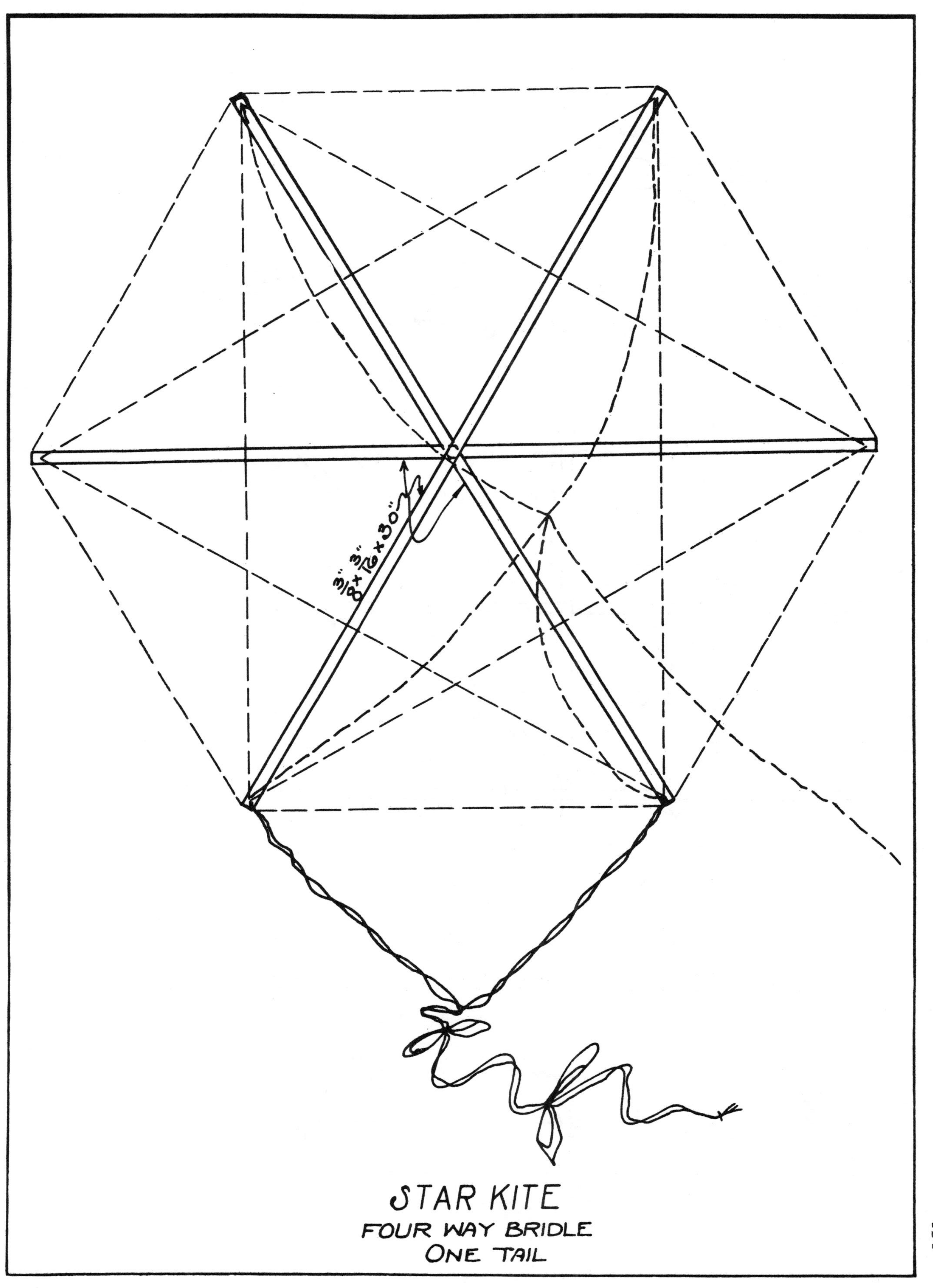

Plate 120.

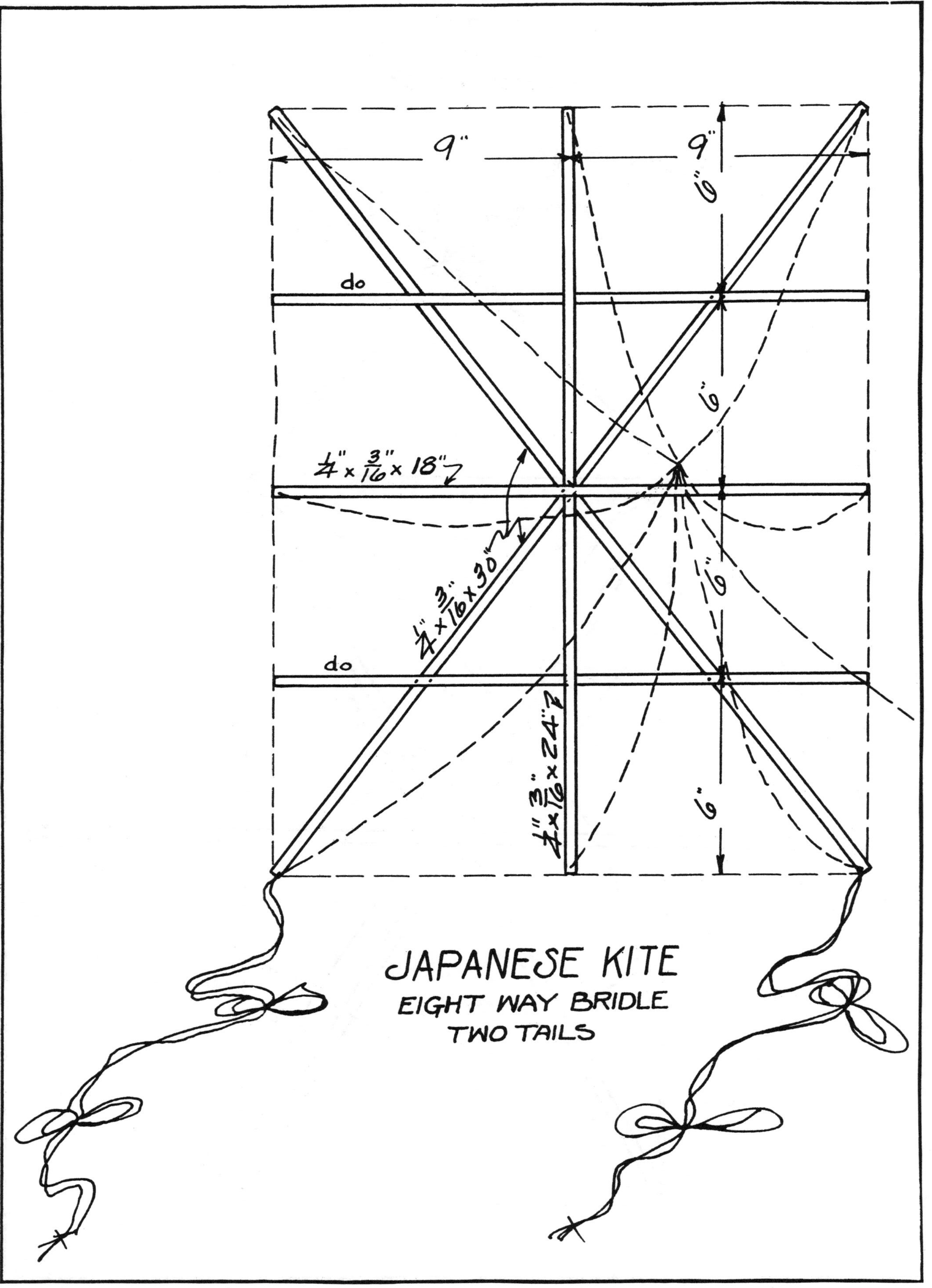
9"
9"
6"
6"
6"
6"
do
¼" x 3/16" x 18"
¼" x 3/16" x 30"
do
¼" x 3/16" x 24"
JAPANESE KITE
EIGHT WAY BRIDLE
TWO TAILS

Plate 121.

INDEX